ABOUT THE AUTHOR

*P*AMMI HAYLETT was born in Scotland during the Second World War. As a child she suffered physical and mental abuse at the hands of her father, and even in adulthood was under the impression that this was how most men behaved.

Attending church on a Sunday and joining church activities as a child, at first was an escapism from the torment of her very non-Christian family, but over the years she became more and more aware that God was playing a very large part in her life. A bit of a loner but not from choice, she found herself writing, in particular, poetry. She had her first poem published in a school magazine at the age of 12.

Living in sixties London, God was far from her thoughts. She married and was blessed with three wonderful children but apart from Christmas, Weddings and Funerals, as a family they did not go to church. After 12 years, the marriage started to fall apart. It was only at the end of a very acrimonious divorce five years later that, totally broken, she asked the Lord to come back into her life.

From that moment things changed dramatically. Still hit by adversity – cancer, redundancy and death of a beloved – but now, with God's presence in her life, each negative turned into a positive.

In 2001 she had her first book of children's poetry *ANIMAL TENNIS AND OTHER POEMS* published, all the proceeds of which were given to Help the Hospices, and other charities for children.

Encouraged by her Bible Study Group she decided to share her "Godly" experiences with others. Pammi's autobiography *WALKING ON EGGSHELLS* is just that.

By the same author

ANIMAL TENNIS AND OTHER POEMS

Pammi Haylett

WALKING ON EGGSHELLS

NEW BOOTS PRESS
CHICHESTER

First published in 2009 by
NEW BOOTS PRESS
E-mail : newbootspress@yahoo.co.uk

Copyright © Pammi Haylett 2009

The right of Pammi Haylett to be identified as the author
of this work has been asserted by her in accordance
with the Copyright, Designs and Patents Act 1988

A catalogue record for this book
is available from the British Library

All rights reserved. No part of this publication may be
reproduced, stored in a retrieval system, or
transmitted at any time or by any means electronic,
mechanical, photocopying, recording or otherwise,
without the prior permission of the publisher.

ISBN 978-0-9541066-1-4

Produced and designed by members of
THE GUILD OF MASTER CRAFTSMEN
EVERGREEN GRAPHICS
11 The Drive, Aldwick, West Sussex PO21 4DU
Cover background photograph by David Haylett
Book Design and Typesetting by Cecil Smith
Typeset in Minion

JIGSAW PRINT PRODUCTION LTD
Forum House, Stirling Road, Chichester, West Sussex PO19 7DN

*Ask, and you will receive;
seek, and you will find;
knock, and the door
will be opened to you.*

LUKE 11 VERSE 9.

CONTENTS

INTRODUCTION   9

PART ONE
Ask, and you will receive   11
    1. The Hand Of God   13

PART TWO
Seek, and you will find   35
    2. Moving On   37
    3. The Power Of Prayer   55
    4. A Special Time   59
    5. Andrew's Story   65

PART THREE
Knock, and the door will be opened to you   71
    6. A Time To Say Goodbye   73
    7. Amazing Grace   89
    8. Glory Glory Hallelujah   103
    9. How Great Thou Art   109
    10. God Works In Mysterious Ways   115
    11. The Family Secret   122

EPILOGUE   128

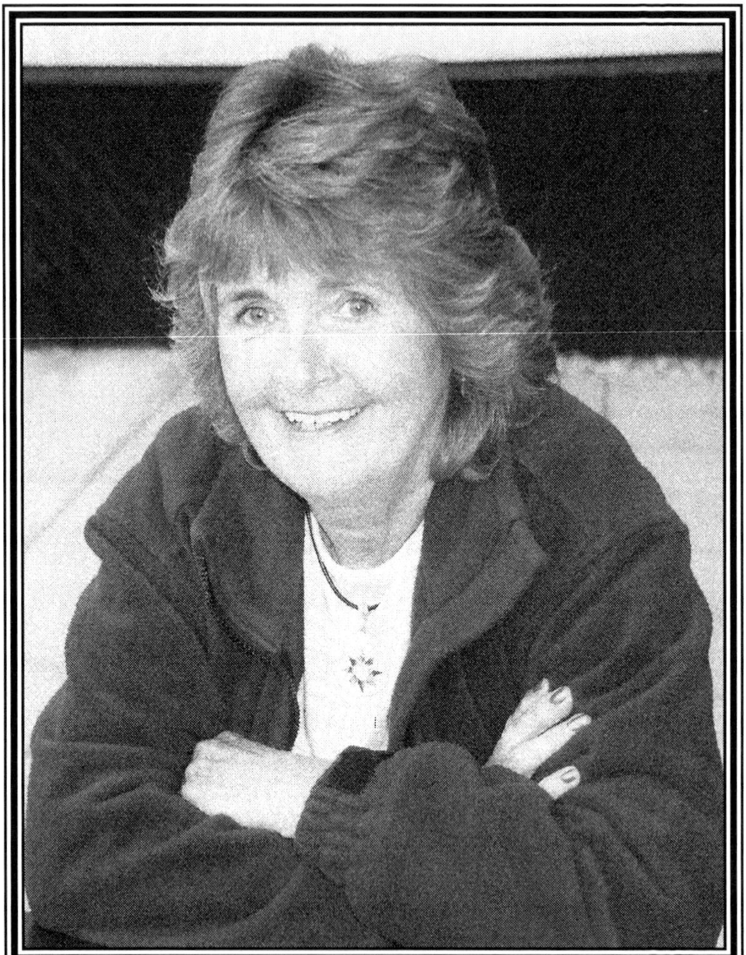

INTRODUCTION

*Ask, and you will receive;
seek, and you will find;
knock, and the door will
be opened to you.*

Luke 11 verse 9.

I feel so honoured and humbled that God has listened to me and touched my life in so many ways. I now want to share my experiences – my witness to the presence of God in my life. If I can encourage one person to read this autobiography, be comforted and think more about what the Lord can do, I shall have done what I set out to do. Having lived through the horrors of childhood abuse, breakdown of a marriage, cancer, death of a beloved and more, yet still found the positives with the Lord's help, I am now telling the tale so that others may find consolation and seek the Lord.

Pammi Haylett

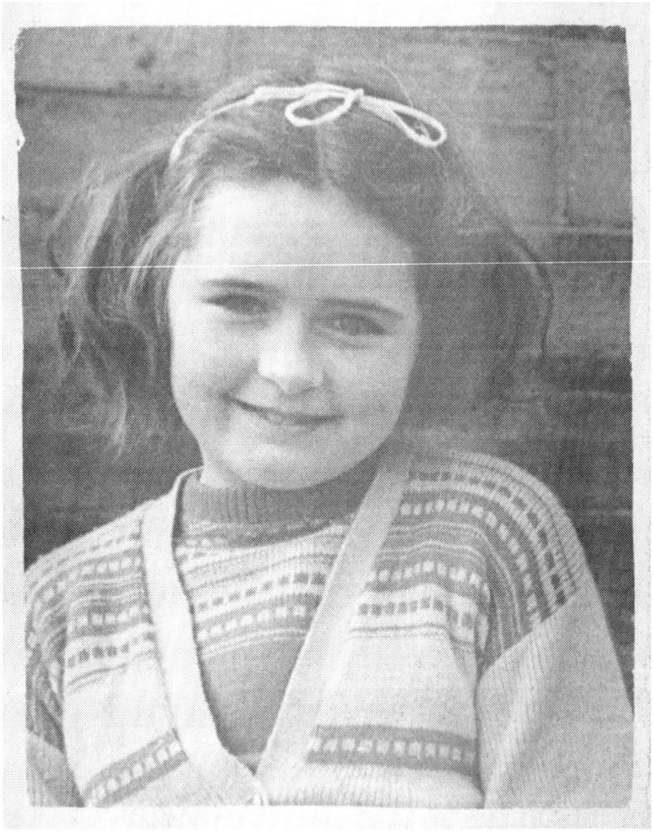

WALKING ON EGGSHELLS

PART ONE

*Ask, and
you will receive*

1

THE HAND OF GOD

*"Please God, come back into my life
and help me."*

Little did I know the joy that was to come from those words, uttered in despair, on that Saturday morning in early September 1985.

It was a plea from the back of a church. I was attending the Wedding Service of a friend's daughter. It was only a last minute decision to go as, a wedding, let alone a church, was the last place I wanted to be, given my unhappy state.

After twelve years of marriage everything had gone horribly wrong and it had taken another five years of very acrimonious divorce proceedings before an end was in sight. That morning sitting in the church, I wept, selfishly, not with tears of joy for the bride but with tears for me. Seventeen years ago this had been me, taking my vows and it had all gone horribly wrong. Totally engulfed by my misery, – the feelings of loss, guilt that I hadn't helped to make it work and the desperate feeling of loneliness, were all wrapped up in the parcel. Then, through the tears I heard myself praying,

*"Please God,
come back into my life and help me".*

I really meant it.

When I was a child, I used to escape to church. My father and mother had no faith and religion was scorned upon. My father abused me physically and mentally and my mother was too weak to stand up to him so, on a Sunday whilst they were busy running an hotel, I escaped to my sanctuary – the local church, eventually joining the choir and taking part in the Church Amateur Dramatic Society. During the Summer I liked nothing better than to get down on to the beach and join the CSM – Church Seaside Mission. Looking back I can see that God already had a hand on my shoulder guiding me through the abuse to a safe corner in my life. My grandparents also encouraged me to attend church, when I visited them in Glasgow during school holidays. Those school holidays; where I could get away from the abuse to the warmth of their love and understanding, were the only times that I can remember with pleasure. Despite having brothers and a sister, it was a pretty lonely, desperate childhood.

My lovely, understanding grandmother died when I was in my teens. It was her dying wish that I get away from my father so, with my mother's blessing and co-operation, this is exactly what happened. I often think back and wonder how much my mother must have suffered at the hands of my father and at my sudden departure. I never found out what he did to her physically, but we had enforced no contact for nearly two years. But there I was, at the ripe old age of 16, joining my grandfather in Glasgow to be his housekeeper, whilst he, in return, was to pay to further my education at a local Ladies College.

Already God was lifting me out of the misery of my home life and, although at the time,

I didn't appreciate "the hand of God",

on reflection I can see He was there at every twist and turn. My life changed enormously. My grandfather taught me to cook using my grandmother's recipes, some of which I still use to this day, and I soon got into a routine of doing housework, attending college, preparing meals and enjoying myself. I joined a local Tennis Club and Youth Group and soon had a social life beyond my furthest dreams. The most outstanding thing in my life by now was that the fear had gone. Returning home each day was a pleasure and held none of the terror that had been with me throughout the years of living with my father.

During my time at the college, I found there was a church nearby which I started to attend. You can imagine how surprised I was to find, much to my delight, that the Church Minister had in fact ministered my baptism. That I had been baptised at all, was indeed a miracle and only came about because my Grandparents had had the good grace to organise this for my six month old sister and myself, when I was four. It was during the war so the Minister had performed the baptism at my grandparent's house. Now here I was re-united with this great man once again, some 12 years later.

When he suggested I might like to be confirmed I was delighted, attended the confirmation classes and was duly confirmed by him. The Life Boys, the younger version of the Boys' Brigade, were looking for a leader and soon I was involved with the group once a week.

In 1969, my much-loved grandfather died after a short illness. He had struggled with the death of my grandmother for nearly four years but without his beloved May, nothing was ever the same for him again. Having got through a bout of pneumonia he then had to be admitted to hospital for gall bladder problems and he finally gave up. Despite only being in his mid Sixties, the will to fight on, without my grandmother, wasn't there.

I was heartbroken. He had been the one person in my life whom I knew loved me and now he was gone. By now I was working as a junior typist for a firm of Chartered Accountants but earning very little. The question of whether, at 20, I should return home was never mentioned. Although I had finally been re-united with my mother, over the telephone, I hadn't actually seen her for nearly four years. My father apparently had told everyone I had deserted the family. Unbeknown to me the hotel they owned had gone into bankruptcy, no doubt something to do with his drinking problem and my mother, unable to stand up to him, had gone along with his story. Now, faced with her father's death we had to meet. It was a very tearful reunion. I didn't go to the funeral, partly because I was too scared of seeing my grandfather in a coffin and partly because I was very scared of meeting my father again.

My future was in the balance, what to do now? There was no invitation to go back and live at home but in any case I would have refused. The solution came from my grandparents' next-door neighbour, Mrs Gardner.

Dear Mrs Gardner had taken in male lodgers for many years; now she was going to succumb to her biggest dread and take in a female lodger – me. Unfortunately her usual regime of providing board and lodgings for five days a week to a young professional gentleman wasn't quite the same as providing board and lodgings seven days a week to an active 20 year old female. To start with, I had washing. None of her previous boarders had washing as they took all this with them when they went home to their wives or mothers at weekends. Then there was food.

Mrs Gardner, whilst she was happy to cook five evening meals a week, suddenly having to provide lunch and dinner at weekends was too much for her. So we came to a compromise. She would provide my usual breakfast of cereal and toast on a Saturday morning and a light supper in the evening, usually a salad. On Sundays, I could have a cooked breakfast and an evening meal. I wasn't allowed to use her kitchen and with very little money, lunch on a Saturday was inevitably a pie or sandwiches. The local dairy, which we now call delicatessens, would make me a ham roll on a regular basis. However, Sunday was different. The shops were closed and so to get round the hunger I stayed in bed till midday. Breakfast then became lunch and at 6 p.m. I had my evening meal. Unfortunately, because of this my church attendance began to slip away. Resourceful as ever, I got a job in a hat shop on a Saturday afternoon and babysat to make enough money to pay for any extras, as my salary just about covered my lodgings and bus fares to work.

Just before my 21st Birthday, the dear lady decided she had had enough and asked me to leave. I think the responsibility was too much for her and I don't blame her at all. Often when babysitting on a Friday or Saturday night I broke her curfew of 10.30 p.m. and didn't return until well after midnight. As she felt it her duty to wait up for me, (she couldn't quite come to grips with the fact that a babysitter can't actually dictate what time the family return), we had had a few disagreements about this and it was therefore time to move on. Looking back I can see her anxiety – in those days we walked everywhere and I often walked home from babysitting after midnight – I wouldn't do it now but in those days it seemed quite normal.

✳ ✳ ✳ ✳

My next lodging house was an experience I would not wish to have again. My landlady was one of the reasons we Scots have a "mean" tag hung on us. It was a cold house and the only way we could keep warm was by huddling round her kitchen fire. This was only lit, when she was at home and we were only allowed into the kitchen if invited. On such days we ended up with red heat marks on the front of our legs and freezing calves and bottoms.

Within a month of my moving into bleak house, as it became known, another girl, Alison, took up lodgings in what would have been the landlady's sitting-room, so the kitchen was then the only shared room apart from the bathroom.

We were allowed one bath a week. From war days the ring around the bath, depicting the maximum amount of water we could use, had stayed. Our Landlady would often hover round the bathroom door to make sure this rule wasn't abused. Sitting in the bath the water didn't even cover my legs so you can imagine how quickly we bathed – to this day the habit of getting in and out of the bath or shower quickly, still remains.

The gas supply to the cooker was another issue. A pipe running the supply of gas to the cooker was situated down the side of the small kitchen window. On this pipe there was a tap, which could be closed or turned on to free the gas supply to the cooker. This was always set at half-mast. She couldn't seem to grasp that with less gas coming through it took twice as long for the kettle to boil. Pies had to be heated in the frying pan, as we were not allowed to use the oven. There was no fridge. We shared a small cupboard with a mesh frontage to keep the flies out which was situated in the hall. With the house being so cold, milk rarely turned sour.

However, on the plus side, I was reconnected with my church, which was about a 25 minute walk from the lodgings. The church was a warm safe place in more ways than one and a lot nicer than lying in bed trying to keep warm on a Sunday.

However, after one very cold winter we decided we had had enough. Alison left before me and just as I was thinking of giving the landlady notice, I managed to disgrace myself, by throwing up all over the bedclothes and bedroom floor. Like magic the horrified landlady appeared in the doorway. Unsympathetically she insisted I clean up there and then, which was probably fair enough but the fact that I was then admitted to hospital for an emergency appendicectomy, didn't wash with her and I was told to find alternative accommodation. She even came into hospital to collect her rent for that week. Parting was no sweet sorrow.

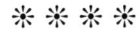

✼ ✼ ✼ ✼

By now I had had my fill of 'digs' and decided to look for a bedsitter. They were pretty easy to come by in those days but not in the area I wanted, or at least not at a price I could afford. Then I found the perfect room in a large flat. It was in a tenement building in a not very salubrious area of Glasgow, but it was love at first sight and I could just about afford it. There were buses nearby which took me to the vicinity of my work place, local shops for food shopping but most of all I loved the room. It was big with a huge mirror between two large windows, which made the room look even bigger. The sun was streaking through the windows the day I went to see it, even now that is how I remember it, a room filled with sunshine.

There was a gas fire, which gave out enough heat to fill the room and a small alcove with a washhand basin and a cooker. It was sparsely but adequately furnished with a bed, wardrobe, two chairs and a table. Not a lot, but to me it was heaven, despite its shabby appearance. I was oblivious to the large gap between my room and the room next door where the plumber had forgotten to make amends when he knocked a hole in the wall whilst putting in a new washbasin, or to the shared bathroom with a constantly dripping tap or the broken pane of glass in the front door.

The night after I moved in I had a bit of a fright. I was awoken to the sound of hammering and realised that the gap in the wall was growing as the two rather dubious young men in the room next door to me, thought they might join me. Fortunately, the landlord was on the premises and sent them packing. The gap was fixed and for the next three years I lived in perfect harmony with the other tenants. For a while these were mostly male students, training to be Doctors, Vets, Scientists, a Teacher and a Butcher and his mate. They were all great fun and treated me like a sister. Many times we sat up into the wee small hours, drinking tea and putting the world to rights. One Student, "Mousey" I will always remember with fondness, as my love of classical music now is due to his consistently loud playing of classical pieces and in particular Chopin's 2nd Piano Concerto. The doors used to rattle when it reached its crescendo. Then I had the good fortune to have a young female teacher, Janet, move next door and we became the best of friends.

The only downside of the move was that it was too far from my church.

I attended the nearest church but it wasn't a friendly church, and so I gave up going for a while, except at Christmas and Easter, besides other things were taking over.

Every Saturday afternoon, I donned my tennis clothes and made my way to the tennis club. It was a very sociable club. I managed to get into the teams and most Saturday evenings there was a dance with a live band in the clubhouse.

I had my first date and started going out regularly with him. He had the most endearing parents who virtually adopted me and each Sunday I was invited for supper. Most of the joy on those Sunday evenings was after supper, when we would adjourn to the front room where his father would sit and play the piano. This man's talent was amazing. Without music he could play virtually anything from Jazz to the Classics and, of course, many, many well beloved hymns, often jazzed up, which seemed almost sacrilegious, but today would be very welcome in our Evangelic Churches.

Much to the joy of his parents, we got engaged just after my 23rd Birthday, I still don't know quite why I agreed to the engagement, as he had a tendency to lash out at me especially when he had been drinking but I was in a routine and needed the comfort and affection of his parents. I think I also thought that this was what most men did. He also had a nasty tendency to make fun of me for a cheap laugh in front of friends but again, although I was very unhappy about it, his parents had such a hold over me, I couldn't give them up. Fortunately our engagement came to an abrupt end when I found out he was cheating on me.

A year later I fell deeply in love.

✳ ✳ ✳ ✳

My landlord also took in boarders in one of the interconnecting houses. Each Saturday morning, I took my rent money to him. He would be in his large kitchen preparing or serving breakfasts. Sometimes I had to hang around until he was finished cooking, then out would come his big rent book. He always insisted on checking the rent money and giving us a receipt. It was during this time that I got to know a few of his lodgers, one in particular, Patrick. Patrick was an Officer in the Royal Navy, and he asked me out time and time again. I wasn't so inclined but eventually I agreed to go on a double date – he would bring a friend and I would bring my flatmate and good friend Janet.

Looking out of the window on the big day, I saw Patrick, walking down the road with a very tall, rather gorgeous looking chap – "Janet, you can have Patrick, I rather fancy the tall guy. I will call him No.1" I told her. So my romance, and indeed her romance with Patrick, materialised and I realised that what I had felt for my fiancé was nothing in comparison to this new, overwhelming feeling of joy and happiness.

✵ ✵ ✵ ✵

I was walking on air. Our romances continued; it was indeed a happy time for us all. A couple of months later, the ship, to which both chaps was attached, was Commissioned and sailed for the South of England, taking them with her.

We kept in touch by letter and the occasional phone call. The boys returned, at separate times, to see us, travelling up to Glasgow by train for long weekends and I travelled to Portsmouth to be with No. 1. During the summer holidays, Janet gave up her room and moved back to the country to be with her parents. We kept in touch by phone but it wasn't the same and I missed her greatly, especially as we had been able to console each other, when we missed the 'boys'. Loving letters and occasional phone calls continued to come from No 1.

Then, one day, I received the letter we all dread. This was different, No 1 was writing from hospital where he had been rushed in with a stomach ulcer. Perhaps the severity of his condition was the trigger factor but whatever the reason, he wrote to me and explained it was time to tell the truth – he was married! I was devastated.

The evening of the day I got the letter I went on my own to see the Eddie Duchin Story in the local cinema. As the haunting music filled me with emotion, I cried all the way through the film. In his letter, No 1 stated he was separated from his wife – well he would be if he was at sea – but naive as I was in those days, I believed him, and mistakenly believed that he was trying to get a divorce and someday we would be together.

⁂ ⁂ ⁂ ⁂

I moved to London, partly to be nearer to No 1 but also it was time to move on job-wise. By now I was working as a PA to the Branch Manager of a large Industrial Company. There were only four of us working in the Regional office, but much as I enjoyed my working environment and the people with whom I was working, I was ready for change. The opportunity arose when a job as PA to one of the Directors at Head Quarters in London was advertised. My trip to London for the interview dispelled any doubts I might have had about leaving Scotland and I was over the moon when I was offered the job.

I found a dear little bed-sitter in North London and settled happily into my new lifestyle. I joined the local tennis club and spent most of my weekends there.

For a while, No 1 and I continued to see each other. He would visit me in London every four to five weeks and occasionally I would go to Portsmouth. More and more I had nagging doubts about what was actually going on. We didn't seem to be moving forward and I began to wonder if he really was separated. Another shock was in store for me.

We were staying at a friend's flat in Portsmouth. No. 1 had gone off to work for a couple of hours, leaving me to tidy up the breakfast things. Beside his friend's phone, on the kitchen breakfast bar, was a Christmas shopping list and casually, as one does, I looked to see what he was buying his friends. They were interesting presents. Then I got to "families". Beside No. 1s name there was the name of a woman, under that, his son's name (He had told me at some stage that he had a son) and then a girl's name, next to which was 'teddy bear'. Now the brain was working overtime – if he had a young daughter, then she must have been conceived whilst we were having our, what can now only be called, "affair". It was one of those heart-stopping moments. I didn't say anything when he returned. We went Christmas shopping. Passing the toys, he hesitated in front of the dolls and I knew then for sure that he had been deceiving me.

Later that day I tackled him. He stood up very well to my questions – his wife was only just pregnant when he met me. It was all a mistake and her way of making him stay. He was a convincing liar and I wanted to believe him – the relationship continued.

❋ ❋ ❋ ❋

It was now four years since we met. No 1 left the Navy, got a job abroad and our relationship came almost to a halt, or so I thought. Three months later, just as I was settling into life in London without him, and just about to go out on a date, he re-appeared.

He had given up, or may have been made to give up, the job abroad and was back in this Country. However things were different for me and I realised that what we had had was dying, if not already dead. My trust in him had completely gone besides which, my priorities were changing and I knew we couldn't continue. It was just choosing when to finish it. As he was living in digs up North our weekends together were few and far between. I was beginning to feel broody and knew that what I really wanted was a family life and I certainly wasn't going to find it with him.

THE HAND OF GOD

✼ ✼ ✼ ✼

I had a pretty active social life. Being part of a good tennis club in London gave me lots of opportunity to make friends. December 1968 I was at a party in Hampstead when somewhere from one of the rooms in the flat, I could hear this deep, sexy voice and something within me stirred. I decided to find out to whom the "voice" belonged, when in walked this man carrying a tray of nibbles. He had a nice face, and was very smartly dressed in blazer and flannels. The voice didn't quite match this, not handsome but not unattractive man, but I was captivated. Some time later we sat on the floor chatting – well, he did most of the chatting as I was quite shy in those days. He was a journalist with a major Airline magazine and was very funny. I enjoyed his company and his chat up lines and was quite despondent when it was time to leave and he hadn't asked me for my phone number.

Another party loomed. My tennis partner and her sister decided to hold a pre-Christmas housewarming party "Are you bringing Sailor boy?" She asked.

"No, he's up North somewhere and I have to finish with him. I need a new life," I replied.

"Well bring someone" she said.

"But I don't know anyone other than tennis people and you have asked all of them" was my response.

"What about that guy, what was his name, Chris, the one you met a couple of weeks ago at Virginia's party – ask him!"

Did I dare? Finally I plucked up courage to get his phone number from Virginia.

Stuttering badly I managed to blurt out the words of invitation.

"A party – what sort of party? Is it a pyjama party?

Should I bring my pyjamas?" he quipped.

He agreed to come but it was a strange evening. Chris followed me everywhere. Whilst feeling flattered at all the attention I was receiving from him, it was all a bit overwhelming, and I wasn't sure whether I wanted it or not, especially when he tried to keep me to himself on the dance floor. As I was staying overnight with my friends I was quite relieved when it was time for him to go home.

However the next day when Chris rang and asked me out I was very happy to go. It was Christmas Eve and I was catching the train to Scotland. We went out for a sumptuous dinner and he waved me on to the train. Most of that holiday, I thought about Chris. He was funny and there was something very endearing about him. I knew I wanted to see him again and I knew that it was time to finish for once and for all with No 1. As I had left, Chris gave me a little Christmas Present to be opened on Christmas Day. I can't say I was over impressed with a stuffed butterfly in a case but it's the thought that counts.

❋ ❋ ❋ ❋

No 1 was coming to stay on my return from Scotland. As always my heart leaped when I saw him but I knew now that this was only physical and the relationship could not go on. Even with all this in my head I spent one more night with him. The next morning, despite his protestations of undying love for me, the sadness, and the tears in his eyes, I stood strong and finished it forever. It was New Year's Eve.

Thank goodness I hadn't slept with Chris. A week later I had to visit my GP who confirmed I had picked up a sexually transmitted disease, obviously No 1's parting gift to me. How could I have been so stupid as to have believed him for all those years when even at the end there must have been someone else.

✸ ✸ ✸ ✸

My spirits were low. Chris hadn't rung me and I was very lonely. I had moved out of my sweet little London bed sit into a bigger one and I didn't like it. Finally in desperation I rang Chris's number.

"Battersea Dog's Home" said the voice.

"Can I speak to Chris, please?" I said. Chris had already told me that his flat mate used to answer the phone pretending to be a Chinese Take Away or Battersea Dog's Home. There was a pause and a lot of giggling before I heard his flatmate calling

"Chris, your Mum's on the phone," more giggling including female laughter.

I can't remember much about that conversation except that Chris informed me he was about to go skiing but he would give me a ring when he came back.

A few days later, a letter arrived from Chris, in which he told me was going skiing with his girlfriend. Great – are there any men out there who can be trusted? How I got through the next few weeks I don't know. I moved into another bed-sit in the same building and then found it had bedbugs. I think I must have been at my lowest ebb at that time. I don't remember praying but it is more than likely that I did. I got a bad case of bronchitis and was confined to bed with the bedbugs.

A month passed and I was able to move back to my old address albeit a different room. Things were on the up. The new room was bigger and better than my tiny bed-sit and I settled in very quickly. Then another letter arrived from Chris. This time he told me that he had made a great mistake. I was the one… he desperately wanted to see me. Cautiously we met up and from then he wooed me. He took me to some fantastic places, the best restaurants and several times I went with him when he was air testing small aeroplanes; it was all very exciting.

Six weeks later he asked me to marry him. He also asked me to keep it a secret for a few months whilst people got used to me being with him. He also wanted to keep it a secret from his mother – maybe I should have seen the warning signs then – but I didn't. Finally in June we announced to the world that we were getting married in August.

At Chris's insistence, we travelled to Scotland so that Chris could meet my parents. Chris still believed in the old-fashioned habit of asking one's father for his daughter's hand in marriage. The fact that the only relationship I had with my parents for years was just chats on the phone to my mother, was no excuse for Chris and so we went up one weekend. That was probably one of the most difficult things I have ever done. I had no idea how my father would behave and I was very scared. Our stay was short, we took them out for a meal, Chris spoke to my father who made some throw away remark about it being about time, and we left early the next morning.

Chris's mum was next on the list. Her first re-action to our news was to ask why we were doing things so quickly, was I in some sort of trouble?

That weekend I also discovered that during Chris's skiing trip with his previous girlfriend, he had asked her to marry him. She had turned him down, and in his desperation to get married, I had become "the one".

❊ ❊ ❊ ❊

THE HAND OF GOD

The August Wedding Day passed in a sort of dream. My mother, who was supposed to be travelling from Scotland with my two Aunts, did not arrive and when I finally spoke to her I realised from her unspoken words that my father had forbidden her to come. A dear friend from the tennis club gave me away at the church ceremony and we had a buffet lunch at a local hotel.

At 6 p.m. as we were about to depart from the wedding scene, my new mother-in-law threw herself at my husband and begged him not to leave her -sadly he never did cut himself off from her ties and for all of our marriage she stayed a dominant figure in our lives. I have since thought many times that had our marriage vows said "forsaking all others, except my mother" our marriage might have lasted longer.

Sadly, it wasn't only his mother that was the problem. The laughter turned to anger.

Chris had always been inclined to dominate me but now this was more and more in evidence and there was no turning back.

I wasn't allowed to choose what we bought for our home, I had no say in colour schemes and any offer of help from me with painting or decorating was always turned down. He was a perfectionist. Meals had to be first class always with meat and two veg. of the right colour and generally cooked to his mother's recipes. This wasn't a bad thing as I think I became quite a good cook in that time.

At first it was easy to go along with him, especially when I became pregnant, first with a son, then two daughters and I threw myself into being a good mother, trying not to believe that the marriage was not what it should have been.

Chris was away a lot of the time. He had a new job, which took him all over the world, for long periods of time, and so, in lots of ways those early years with the children was spent almost as a lone parent.

When Chris returned from his long trips he found it difficult to settle down to being tied down with a family. He would disappear to do his "own thing", sometimes going out but most of the time, it was to the study not to be disturbed. Feeling the frustration of an unsuccessful marriage he took to not only throwing cruel words at me but started to lash out. Then I realised that something else was going on.

❈ ❈ ❈ ❈

Now the long trips were becoming less frequent. He was still going away but mostly in the UK and so he was around more.

Our youngest was just over a year, when Chris suggested we take an Autumn weekend break in the Lake District. I was delighted and was hopeful that maybe we could get things back on the right road. By now I assumed that most marriages were like ours and had accepted that romantic marriages only happened in books.

On the way to the Lake District , Chris stopped at a phone box – "Must ring the office, make sure everything is OK". During our weekend away, not only did he ring "the office" but "the office" rang him by way of his secretary, at least six times. Were warning bells ringing – no! Christmas came and he worked every day including Boxing Day and New Year's Day, despite the office being closed. We were invited to dinner at his secretary's house, very cosy. Again, warning bells – no! I should have been more astute when he said he was taking his secretary on a trip to Aberdeen then America but sometimes the brain does not want to believe what it is hearing or seeing – you would think mine, with its previous history, would have learned but apparently not.

The children occupied most of my time and blotted out any thoughts that my husband might be seeing another woman.

Then one evening it all became apparent. We were to take a customer out for dinner. Chris asked if he could bring his secretary. He asked me!! After a bit of hesitation I said "fine". That evening I have never felt so uncomfortable. The client and I might just as well have not been there, so strong was the chemistry between Chris and his secretary. I am sure they spent at least twenty minutes looking into each other's eyes – it was awful. After the meal when we were about to leave, she removed an imaginary hair from my husband's coat and said, "Christmas went on for ever and ever, didn't it Chris?" The penny finally dropped and went straight to the slot. My husband was having an "affair". That evening I confronted him with a "her or me". She left the office within two weeks of the ultimatum. Looking back I realise the breakdown of our marriage was my fault too. I had been so wrapped up in my children, I hadn't gone on trips with him when he asked, nor had I noticed that things weren't as they should be and had made no attempt to work at our marriage to save it. My neglect of attention to my husband certainly contributed to his presumed adultery.

✻ ✻ ✻ ✻

My confidence and self-esteem were low but my love for the children was so great that for a while I tried to make everything work. I even went to Relate and to "help me" he came too. The marriage lasted two more years.

Then it all started up again. I was standing up for myself more and more resulting in constant arguments and occasionally he would lash out at me. Chris seemed to be getting more aggressive. On one occasion, provoked by me, he broke two eggs on top of my head. Well they do say raw egg is good for your hair and I take responsibility for the incident as I provoked him.

This was not the only physical incident but I suffered more from the lashing of his tongue. Friends tried to make him see that what he was saying to me in public as well as in private was unnecessarily cruel but he couldn't stop. Several times I told him I was going to leave him if he continued but each time he just laughed it off. I was too stupid etc.

Finally after yet another physical incident, I snapped, moved to another bedroom and started divorce proceedings.

❋ ❋ ❋ ❋

Chris was in denial. As far as he was concerned, there was nothing wrong with our marriage and he defended the case. Then followed five years of hell, whilst we went through all the divorce proceedings. Never have I been so humiliated or so torn apart. My Solicitor wanted more and more evidence to support my claim of "breakdown of marriage" there were no secrets, our sex life was torn into shreds along with every small incident that I could recall. It was ghastly but an inner strength kept me going until finally we separated fully and I was able to move into a small, terrace house with the two girls. By now Chris was living with a woman he had met some three years previously. He had only finally agreed to the divorce on the grounds that he could have care and control of our son and that I would only take one third of the estate. Despite my Solicitor's protestations, I agreed to this, so worn down by the continuous battle over money and all the nasty things that can go with divorce all I wanted was "out".

The divorce finally went through and now, more than twenty years later, I am happy to say we are quite good friends.

❋ ❋ ❋ ❋

And so it came about that I was sitting in the Church that day praying for God to come back into my life. Reading through the previous pages I realise that

He never actually left my side.

He carried me safely through all those trials and tribulations. I had choices and made many mistakes but I realise that He never actually left me but by asking him to come back into my life, I turned the corner and wonderful things were about to happen.

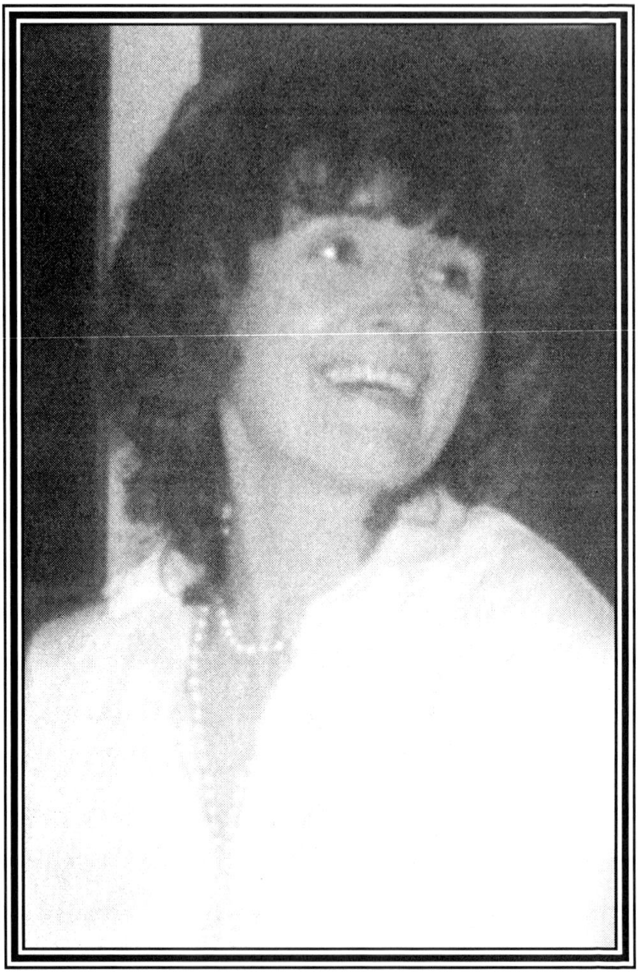

WALKING ON EGGSHELLS

PART TWO

*Seek, and
you will find*

2

MOVING ON

"The Holy Spirit."

Chris and I had separated totally. We sold the family house and with my 40% of the estate, plus a mortgage, I was able to buy a small terrace house about three miles away. From day one I loved the house. It was small but it had everything I needed. A perfect little kitchen, beautifully fitted out, a large living room with ample room to put a dining room table and best of all, a small sunroom extension. Upstairs there were two good-sized bedrooms and a small but adequate third bedroom. Furthermore the small back garden had been laid to patio, which was perfect for a working Mum with little interest in gardening. So many times I counted my blessings and praised the Lord at this time. It was just before the move that the biggest blessing of all came into my life.

⁂ ⁂ ⁂ ⁂

It was about a month before removal day. A friend rang me and asked if I was bringing anyone to the Tennis Club Dinner Dance. At that time I had been going (dragged, I might say) to a singles club and had made a few friends – this was a very interesting experience and certainly not for the feint hearted. The impression it left with me, was that anyone who was not sure about their marriage should try the singles scene for a month and believe me if there was any saving in their marriage they would soon scuttle back. I am sure in this modern day, things have changed with some very good singles clubs, indeed, I was later to find out that this was very much the case. However, in my story, we are in the early eighties and a lot of people did stay in their soured marriages very often working through their problems, so the singles scene was not really a desirable place to be. I digress: back to the tennis club dinner dance – I had thought about taking along one such single gentleman, with whom I had become friendly, but it was only a thought and when my friend then said they were thinking of inviting Luke, an old mutual friend, and would I like to partner him, I jumped at the chance.

Whilst my children were at Junior School, I had become involved with the school Parent Teachers Association and in particular with the amateur theatre productions. Luke was Stage Manager of these productions whilst I used to hide away in the chorus. At the end of each production we would have an after-show party and on each occasion Luke had made a beeline for me as a dancing partner. So, of course, my immediate reaction at the prospect of having him as a partner for the Tennis Club bash was, – 'Terrific, Luke can dance'.

I had learned many months previously that Luke's wife had left him, leaving him with his two sons and whilst I had, at the time, been tempted to ring and offer him solace, I didn't, really because I didn't know him well enough and also because I too was still feeling vulnerable. We had always been accompanied to the after-show parties with our spouses and really only knew each other through the productions and the little bit of dancing we had enjoyed.

It seemed that Luke had likeminded thoughts and a few days later he phoned me and asked if he might take me to the Dinner Dance. That was the beginning of an amazing friendship. Again I thanked God for bringing him into my life and prayed that the friendship would continue.

✳ ✳ ✳ ✳

I moved into my little house as planned. I will never forget that magical moving morning. There was an early morning mist, with the sun trying to peep through the clouds. Our piano was sitting at the top of our drive, waiting to be put on the van, when suddenly I could hear it being played and looking through the window, I saw my daughter Grace, sitting arms outstretched playing Beethoven's 'Fur Elise', what an enchanting moment. Friends helped me move to save costs and what fun it was to sit on the floor eating sandwiches, drinking sparkling wine and pretending it was champagne. It was indeed a day for celebration. Chris had already moved out and in with his new girlfriend, my son was at boarding school, and although Luke was now on the scene, he was away on business.

So the girls and I and a few friends made several trips in cars and finally we closed the doors on the old, unhappy house. A few days later Luke came and laid some carpets, cutting them to size from the old house, old friends joined us in the evening and we celebrated the freedom, the move and my new friend.

✳ ✳ ✳ ✳

Just before Christmas, Grace, was playing her saxophone in a Christmas concert in a local village school hall. Luke accompanied me to the concert and as we were standing singing a carol, I suddenly felt a warm glow sweep through me, with it I experienced a huge sense of peace and an awareness that everything was going to be alright – I now recognise that

*this was God touching me
with the Holy Spirit.*

Although I had now become a regular at church, Luke was a different matter.

His father had trained as a pharmacist but then moved to Africa into Missionary work. Luke was born in Africa and had been brought up in this very religious family. When he came to England to boarding school he continued with his religious beliefs but this had slipped away from him over the years and with the split up with his wife, he had almost become a non-believer. Eventually I was able to get him to come to church with me but it was several months before I could persuade him to take communion.

As the months went by Luke and I became closer and closer and about ten months later he suggested I move in with him. My divorce had gone through very easily, after the five years of acrimony but Luke was still waiting for his divorce, however it seemed mad to be running two homes when we knew we wanted to be together. Our year had been wonderful and we were in love.

My main concern at that time was my children. My son was under the care of his father, with regular visits to me, so there wasn't an issue there. Grace was sixteen and when I told her that I was thinking of moving in with Luke, she showed little sign of emotion. She was very wrapped up in her own world, had a regular boyfriend and worked hard at school and didn't really seem to mind where we were as long as her life could continue without too much disruption.

However, my twelve-year old daughter, Susie, was a different kettle of fish. I knew she liked Luke but I wasn't prepared for her reaction when I told her my news. She was well used to staying at Luke's place as he had prepared a room for the girls in his spacious house, and they were used to staying in the two places. I knew she didn't have problem with that, especially as she found her little room in our house too small. So I was quite shocked when I told her I was thinking of moving in with him. She went very pale then red, as her eyes filled with tears. "But Mum you have just come out of a bad marriage, how do you know it will work this time and what if it doesn't."

I thought hard, she was very important to me but I also had a life and for the first time in years I was happy. I explained all this to her but so that she would know how important she was to me, I asked her to go away and think about it.

"If you really don't want me to move in with Luke, I won't, but if he then decides to stop seeing me and I meet someone else, you might not like him as much. There is no rush, lets talk about it again when you have had time to think."

Bless her – she came back the next morning with her words of wisdom,

"It's alright Mum, I have thought about it and it is OK for you to move in with him." Phew.

I sold my little house virtually overnight for a good price and the girls and I and our two cats moved in with Luke and his two boys just before Christmas. That Christmas was fun. Luke and his sons cooked Christmas lunch and we had parties. Very often the children stayed away with friends at weekends. Luke's boys went to their mother on alternative weekends and my girls were often at sleepovers and had sleepovers with us.

Grace completed her O levels successfully but with the prospect of A levels coming up, Luke and I decided, with his divorce imminent, to start looking for a bigger house so that each child could have their own room.

My dearest son, Andrew, was still at boarding school, spending exeats with his father but we knew the time was coming when he too would be joining us for long holidays, before going on to university.

Luke's divorce came through, and we sold the house. With my capital and his mortgage undertaking we found the perfect house. It had five large bedrooms, three bathrooms, a big kitchen, superb lounge and a dining room with patio doors that when opened filled the house with the scent of the flowering, wisteria. The minute we walked in we knew it had to be ours.

It was a happy house and we all settled in very quickly. In the summer it was a 'full' house. With everyone at home, Luke's two boys and my three children, plus goodness knows how many of their friends, it was a busy time.

Luke asked me many times to marry him. I was very resistant. After all we were happy and I was very scared that getting married again would spoil everything. Finally, I said that if he asked me again, I would say no forever. He stopped then but each day would make some remark like "On that day that I am not allowed to mention!…

❉ ❉ ❉ ❉

By now we were attending church regularly and Luke was

once again taking communion. We were building up a good social life with our joint amateur dramatic friends and with our church friends.

One evening we arranged to meet up with some friends, Michael and Janet, in a Chinese Restaurant. During the course of the evening, Michael, said to me.

"I have some very exciting news for you but you will probably think I am crazy"

Curious I asked "Go on?"

"Well, for the last year or so, I have had this feeling that God is calling me".

I should point out that Michael was on the board of one of the top, successful companies in the UK.

"But what about your job" I asked.

"I have decided to resign and see if I can get into Theological College".

Somehow I knew he would do it, and made all the right encouraging noises. After an unsuccessful first attempt, Michael persisted. He worked as a gardener for a year, and then reapplied. This time he was successful and started his training. Little did I know that

the hand of God was once again on our shoulders.

✳ ✳ ✳ ✳

It was 1988 and the tennis club dance loomed again. This was always to be a special event for us, the anniversary of our first date. We had a table for ten with all our special friends. As the evening wore on and we were getting ready for the inevitable speeches, I saw Luke come in with a lovely bouquet of flowers which I assumed were for our lady chairman. The speeches came and went and people started to get up to dance. Usually we were first on the floor so when

Luke laid his hand on my arm I turned expecting him to ask me to dance.

Instead he said "I think this is now the right time to ask you, Pammi, will you marry me". I was so flabbergasted I started to laugh. "Don't be silly". I continued laughing then I saw him take a small square box from his pocket and put it on the table. One of my friends saw what was happening and before I knew it they were all gathered in front of us, egging Luke on. Luke then went down on his knees and asked me good and proper.

I was stunned, I didn't feel ready for marriage; on the other hand I couldn't let him down, so I said yes. He presented me with the flowers. Champagne was bought, everyone cheered, congratulations were bestowed upon us and we danced. Still I had that sinking feeling that I wasn't ready for this. However when we got home Luke took me in his arms and made everything right by saying "I am not rushing you into marriage. But I feel much happier now we are engaged and I know you will tell me when you are ready, I won't mention it until you do". He stuck to his word and three months later, I woke up one morning and realised how silly I was being – here was a man who totally loved me and I him, so why not get married. That night called for more champagne as we set the date for November.

Our wedding was truly wonderful. Both being divorced we had no option but to have a civil ceremony in the local Register Office but we followed this with a beautiful church blessing and I can remember crying tears of happiness, as I was about to walk down the aisle so proudly with my new husband.

The following year we had the patter of tiny feet as, Tootsie and Sammie our two rescue dogs, joined us. That summer, we had five teenage children, two dogs, two cats and Luke's mother came to stay for a week. I don't know when I have ever felt so exhausted but happy.

As winter approached we started rehearsing for our next show, to be shown the following March. It was to be Sleeping Beauty and I was one of the good fairies. I loved the part and it was good to be doing something different other than chorus.

I was also looking for a change in career.

✳ ✳ ✳ ✳

In my teens, the Ladies College in Glasgow had given me a good grounding in secretarial work and following in my grandfather's footsteps I had spent eight years working as a junior typist then finally as secretary to the Head Partner of a firm of Chartered Accountants. It was boring and looking for a change I had got a job as PA/Office Manager for the Glasgow offices of a large commercial company. The move to London to work for one of the main directors of the company gave me the opportunity to follow my interest in medicine. In Glasgow I had already done First Aid courses and joined the Red Cross. Now I had the opportunity of doing even more First Aid, looking after 200 staff, in the First Aid Department, as part of my job, and doing First Aid shifts at theatres and events around London. This was to give me even more of a thirst for medicine.

Having moved out of London, after my marriage to Chris, I then trained as a school dental nurse, only leaving the job when I became pregnant with Andrew. Pregnant and confined to hospital for 3 months, I was more and more interested in obstetrics. Two more pregnancies followed and it was during the early years following Susie's birth that I had the opportunity to train as an ante-natal teacher. Over 500 births and some eight years later, I gave up teaching to return to work as a school dental nurse. However, after four years, I wasn't enjoying it and was ready to move on again. A job came up as a Medical Secretary for a GP Practice, this also incorporated helping on reception and in the dispensary. It fitted in with the school hours, and so I moved into general practice.

It was during this time that my divorce from Chris went through and Luke appeared on the scene.

I had been there for four years when the GPs started looking for a Manager. Practice Managers were now being employed to take the burden off doctors and to manage staff and budgets. I needed a challenge and felt that this could be of interest, especially as there was a training programme for new Managers.

Following my interview with my Doctors and whilst the Doctors were mulling over the applications, a job came up as Manager of the A& E department at the local hospital. This also appealed to me so I applied. I was called for an interview and to my amazement was offered the job in the hospital almost straight away. I needed time to consider the best route and was given a week.

❋ ❋ ❋ ❋

So here I was with a job decision to make and a delightful part in our Am. Drams play. This was all around my 50th Birthday and like most women throughout our country I was due to have my first mammogram. Somehow I managed to squeeze in an appointment but believed it to be a waste of time, as I didn't have any lumps or bumps and I was really too busy. I didn't enjoy having the mammogram done and was relieved when it was all over, or so I thought. The next morning I had a phone call from the hospital when I heard the words no woman ever wants to hear.

"We would like you to come back for another mammogram." My legs went to jelly as I asked the nurse to repeat what she had just said. An appointment was also arranged to see the Consultant, just in case.

It is one thing working in a medical environment but totally another being a patient. I was scared witless. Luke and I went along together. The wait for the films to be developed and the appointment with the Consultant was probably only half an hour but it felt like hours. She pointed out an area, which was different to the rest, but reassured me that it was probably nothing more than a cyst. However to be on the safe side she indicated I should have a needle biopsy.

Returning home that morning, I asked Luke to make love to me, as I needed to feel like a woman. He lovingly obliged and as we were repairing to the bathroom, the telephone rang. It was my dear boss offering me the position of Practice Manager. There cannot be many people who are offered the job of Practice Manager whilst standing in the nude. Standing there I explained what the Consultant had told me.

"You'll be fine. The job is still yours if you want it." What a lovely man and what a boost for my confidence. I accepted gladly and later that day declined the hospital job.

As we had private medical cover we arranged for the needle biopsy to be done the following week at our local private hospital. I was totally alone when the Consultant Surgeon rang me at home two days later following the biopsy with the result.

"I am really sorry to have to tell you that the lump has proved to be malignant.

Can you come and see me please".

I felt as if I was living in another world, one in which I did not want to take part. Luke took the day off so he could come with me to the appointment. The Consultant was anxious to get me in for surgery as soon as he could but when I explained that I had a part in a show, albeit it was only an amateur dramatic event, and we didn't know what was ahead of us, he agreed to delay the operation by a week so I could perform, as long as I promised to be on his list the Tuesday after the last performance on the Saturday. Luke and I agreed that we would tell no-one until after the last show.

The lump was removed, surrounding tissue and lymph glands. Whilst the lump proved to be malignant, fortunately the surrounding tissue and the lymph nodes were benign.

We didn't tell Grace and Susie what I was having done, merely that I was having a small op and would only be in for a couple of days. Grace was furious with me when she found out.

"Don't do that ever again Mum. Something might have happened to you and we wouldn't have been prepared." Older and wiser, I know she was right.

It all seems to be so simple now but believe me at the time it wasn't.

I went through all the emotions that apparently happen when told you have cancer – disbelief, non-acceptance, fear that you are about to die and anger. As I walked the dogs through a field in the pouring rain one day I shouted at God "Why?" I shouted at my mother who had dared to pass away a few months previously, but of course at that time

I was unaware of God's plan.

Determination got me through; with God's blessing and Luke's total support,

I was back playing tennis within three months and even managed to play in a league tennis match that summer.

As time went on, regular scans showed that everything

was normal. I was put on the drug Tamoxifen for five years. Ideally they would have liked me to have had radiotherapy to the offending breast, but when I went along to be measured I was so hostile to having it that, after discussion with the Oncologist, it appeared that I was very much a borderline case. The lump had been deep, near to my heart and had been removed. With no other spread it seemed it wasn't a cut and dried case that I must have radiotherapy. I chose not to and was out of the door like a shot. Luke was not impressed and wouldn't talk to me for twenty-four hours as he felt I was losing the belts and braces effect.

During this time, my Vicar ran a "healing session" and I decided it was worth a try. With a few others we attended the service. At the appropriate time, Luke took me up to the Altar where the Vicar laid his hand on my shoulder and prayed for me that the cancer had gone. As he prayed, I felt a warm glow sweep through my entire body.

At the end of the five-year period my Consultant Surgeon and the X-rays confirmed that I was totally clear.

✼ ✼ ✼ ✼

Following the cancer scare Luke decided that we needed to get away more often. Both of us were working long hard hours and quite stressed with our commitments. I loved my job but it was tiring, so we decided to have short, frequent breaks away. Buying another small property near the coast seemed a good investment. Hotels were expensive and rooms not always available whereas having something small would mean that we could escape as often as we wanted. After several months of looking around we found the ideal bolthole – a small flat just outside of Chichester. It was perfect and we got into a routine of taking a break every three weeks. We joined the tennis club, went for long walks on the beach, ate at the local Pub and joined in local community events when we could. We made new friends and became very endeared to Chichester.

Then we suffered another blow, Luke was made redundant. Although he was virtually the last person to have to leave the company, he took it personally and badly. The thought of losing our lovely house was foremost in our minds and we went through all the options, one of which was to sell the house and flat and buy a Post Office business, which usually came with house attached. We spent weekends touring the countryside looking at the possibilities but just as we were considering putting in an offer on one in Dorset, Luke was amazingly given another option. One of the Agencies with whom he had been in touch, gave him a very lucrative contract for a year. Although it meant he would be away from home for a few days at a time it was a really good opportunity. It also meant we could stay where we were. How blessed we felt.

It was a good year. We balanced the stress of the jobs with weekends in Chichester. I missed Luke dreadfully on the days and nights he had to spend away but cherished the time we did have together.

Towards the end of his one-year contract, he was approached and asked if he would consider moving to Hamburg to do the next stage of the contract, which would be another year and if that went well there was Spain to consider. We discussed this in detail. Luke was excited about it. If he took the job in Hamburg I would go to. We would find rented accommodation, the only downside being that I would have to give up my job, but at least we would be together.

❋ ❋ ❋ ❋

All was going well. It was just four weeks to D-day, the 1st of

June, when all the work that Luke had been doing over the year culminated into one package and went live. A holiday in Spain was next, before tackling the move to Hamburg.

We spent the weekend at the flat and were leaving early to return home to take part in a tennis tournament, when Luke said he didn't feel too good. His neck was a bit stiff and he felt a bit sick. I offered to cancel the tennis but he said, "No, we are not letting anyone down," but I could see he wasn't himself. We lost the match and when we got home he said he had a headache and still felt sick. It all sounded a bit like migraine and so I gave him some pills and sent him off to bed. He got up during the night and was sick but the next morning he felt a bit better. That week he was working in London but each night, when he returned, he complained of headaches and visual disturbance. It would wear off and next morning he was off to work again. We assumed it was stress.

The following week he had to go to Edinburgh. On both Monday and Tuesday evening when he rang, he complained of headaches – we agreed it was also probably something to do with sitting in front of the computer all day. On the Wednesday he rang me at lunchtime to say he was coming home on the afternoon flight as he was feeling so unwell. I knew then there must be something major going on. Luke was a 'money man' and as he earned his money by the day, there had to be something seriously wrong for him to even consider giving up half a days work. I rang his GP who was also a good friend. He wasn't in the surgery so I rang his wife and told her everything. Luke arrived home at 6 p.m. and his GP arrived five minutes later. He diagnosed cluster headaches, gave him some painkillers and suggested he rest, tension most likely being the cause. A week later and Luke was no better. In fact he was getting worse. He would wake up being sick with a headache then it would go away. He would get up for a few hours but then the sickness and headaches came back. Other doctors came and this was now being diagnosed as cluster Migraines. Stronger painkillers and eventually an injection were prescribed. Nothing touched it.

His GP came with the Senior Partner in the Practice but once again they agreed that, in their opinion, it was just a bad case of cluster migraine.

By the following Tuesday I had had enough. Luke's headaches were getting a lot worse and he was being sick regularly. He would wake at 1 a.m. with a headache, be sick then feel a bit better. The pattern was continuing every 3-4 hours. Taking the bull by the horns I rang the surgery and said I wanted him to see a Neurosurgeon. Although they tried to assure me that this wasn't necessary, I finally got their agreement and using Luke's private health insurance rang the local private hospital, where I had had my operation, and asked for an urgent appointment with the Neurosurgeon, who, as it happened was in clinic that week. The secretary was a bit reluctant but eventually let me speak to the Neurosurgeon. After discussion, he agreed to shuffle his appointments and see Luke the next day. Fifteen minutes into the consultation and he had booked a CT scan. They kept him in overnight for observation and the next day we were given the dreadful news that the scan revealed that Luke had a large tumour nestling in the brain. The next step was to get him into a Neurological hospital for surgery.

The options were London or Oxford. I knew driving through London with a sick man beside me was not an option, so I agreed to take him myself to Oxford. What a journey. With Luke beside me holding his sick bowl and crying out in pain every time we went over a bump in the road, it was a total nightmare. However we got to the John Radcliffe Infirmary and were seen almost straight away by the surgeon on duty – a lovely man. After studying his X-rays he told us that there was some good news. The tumour was operable but the bad news was that he suspected, in layman terms, it was a Glioma. These came in grades from 1-4 and he hoped that it would only be a grade 1, but he wouldn't know that until he had operated.

It was a Saturday morning and the surgeon arranged to perform the operation as soon as he could the following week. That weekend continued to be a nightmare. By now Luke couldn't hold anything down, and nothing they gave him would take away the pain in his head. The surgeon returned and agreed to fit Luke in at the end of his list on the Monday.

Two of my closest friends, who were good Christians, came with me into the hospital on the Monday and we prayed for Luke's recovery whilst he was in Theatre. They left on his return from Theatre and the staff set up a Z-bed in Luke's room so I could stay with him. It was an interesting night, with the grinding and pumping and bleeping of the various machines to which Luke was attached. Every now and then he would call out "Are you there, Pammi" and then "Pammi water please". I was allowed to wet his mouth with little sponges on a stick. At some stage during the night I became aware of a great clattering going on from the room across the corridor. As my brain went into gear, I recognised that the patient in the room opposite was having an epileptic fit. I must have looked quite a sight running down the corridor in my short nightdress to get a nurse.

Two days later and we were confronted with bad news. Pathology confirmed that the tumour was in fact a fast growing tumour, in brief, a Glioma stage IV. Whilst the surgeon had been able to remove the bulk of it, he warned us that the residual piece would grow.

A fortnight later we returned home. However, within three days Luke started being sick again. There was no delay this time. We went straight back to the hospital where he was re-admitted. This time there could be no operation and for the next week he continued vomiting, losing weight rapidly and it was obvious to everyone that he was dying.

Then along came another of those never to be forgotten moments of

the Grace of God.

3

THE POWER OF PRAYER

"Please God give us more time together"

*I*t was all I wanted. I think I knew from the moment of diagnosis that Luke was going to die. I could accept that this was going to happen but what I couldn't accept was the short time we had left.

My friends were wonderful and rallied round to do driving shifts. Someone would take me to the hospital in the morning and someone else would collect me in the evening. This gave me the whole day with Luke. At first I was doing the 40 minute, each way, journey by myself, but driving home each evening in floods of tears, praying for more time together was taking its toll and my family were getting increasingly worried about me, so a rota was drawn up by my friends, to provide me with company and transport.

✳ ✳ ✳ ✳

During Luke's short return home, we had several callers but the one that both of us most remembered was Michael and Janet's son, Mark.

Mark was about 21 and he himself had been in the same hospital having a brain tumour removed, some months previously. When he visited us he had lost all his hair from the chemotherapy but he was so calm and caring, only interested in what Luke was going through. Before he left, he asked Luke if he could pray for him. This was the first time I had ever seen Luke cry. He found it difficult to believe that, after all that Mark had gone through he still retained his strong faith. As he left Mark gave him five letters cut out and held together with a piece of string. The letters made up the word TRUST and to this very day they are glued to the bottom of the mirror that was in our bedroom.

❋ ❋ ❋ ❋

Now we were back in hospital and Luke was slipping away.

> *"Please Lord, give us some more time together."*

This was my constant prayer.

It was Sunday morning. Around 8 a.m. the telephone rang and the Sister in charge of the Ward said the words I had been dreading
"I think you should come in now, I am sorry to say but I think your husband is slipping away".
Just as I replaced the receiver, the doorbell rang and to my amazement the same two friends who had been with me throughout Luke's operation were standing on the doorstop. They had a large family and it was all they could do to get themselves organised for church on a Sunday let alone come and see me.
I told them what had happened and they agreed one of them would take me to the hospital.
"Obviously God planned for us to come and see you this morning", they said, not sounding at all surprised that they

had arrived at just the right moment.

Arriving at the hospital, I was ushered into Sister's office. After asking me to sit down, she took my hand, "I am very sorry to say that Luke is slipping in and out of consciousness and we feel he is very near the end, I just want you to be prepared," she warned me.

That day I sat and held Luke's hand, read to him and just talked about anything that I thought might interest him. He had said my name at one point and that gave me all the strength I needed to keep going but then he had slipped away again and seemed to be in another world.

My friends arrived about 10 o'clock to take me home. The staff insisted that I go. There was nothing I could do and they felt I needed to rest. I recollect asking the Registrar on duty, not to ring me if Luke died during the night. I had already experienced receiving a call of death during the night when my grandfather died and I knew I would lie awake, waiting for the phone to ring. They said they would make a note of it but couldn't promise. However, I was so exhausted I fell into bed and slept till 7 a.m. The moment I awoke, I was on the phone.

"He is in a coma and we don't expect him to last the day." His special nurse informed me. "Come in as soon as you are ready".

Getting dressed, I looked at the rota and saw there was a blank space. Well, I suppose I had better drive myself, I thought; then I remembered Michael. Dear Michael, who had said, "please ring me any time night or day if I can be of help".

I hadn't had to ask him before but now I was glad of his offer. Bless him.

"Of course I will take you to the hospital," he said with his usual chirpiness. "Be with you shortly".

It was a bit of a shock when I opened the door, to see him proudly wearing a dog collar. He had been ordained the day before. In all my sorrow I had completely forgotten and here he was now, tired from all the celebrations but proudly standing on my doorstep.

We stopped at the Nursing Station. "It won't be long now," they said looking at Michael, obviously thinking I had come prepared with my Priest. I looked at Michael and he gave a wry smile. We walked to Luke's room and opened the door. I approached the bed and took Luke's hand.

"Luke, its Pammi" I said. Not a sign so I repeated myself "Luke, its Pammi."

Not a flicker passed his face. No grunt just a peaceful look on his face.

I walked to the window fighting the tears. As I turned round, just for a moment I felt as if I was looking in on a scene and was no longer part of the room. Michael walked over to Luke's bed and took his hand.

"Luke, its Michael," he said quietly. There was a pause and then the most astounding thing happened.

Slowly Luke opened his eyes.

"Why Michael you have been ordained. Congratulations," he said.

❄ ❄ ❄ ❄

From that moment we never looked back. Luke left his coma behind, stopped being sick and, for the next 17 months, we had that precious time together that had been my constant prayer.

God had answered my Prayers.

4

A SPECIAL TIME

*"Thank you Lord for bringing us to
the beginning of this new day."*

❋ ❋ ❋ ❋

The next seventeen months was a mixture of laughter and tears. We learned how to cry together, pray together and, with the new sense of humour with which Luke had suddenly been blessed, laugh together.

❋ ❋ ❋ ❋

"I never tell anyone how long they have got because I don't know, but I would suggest that whatever you planned for the future, you do it now." How wise was Luke's Surgeon. Following his discharge from hospital, an eight-week course of radiotherapy was planned.

Luke's main worry was that, apart from my salary, we now had no other income and we had a very large mortgage. There was nothing for it but to sell the house. We had already put feelers out regarding valuations with Estate Agents when we thought there was a possibility of us going to Hamburg so we picked up where we left off and put the house on the market.

The decision was what to do when we had sold. We had two choices. After paying off our large mortgage, did we move away or buy something in the same area to be near our friends? Although the latter sounded, at first, the best option, when we looked around we realised that anything we could afford would be so small that we would be unable to have the children to stay for long periods or, indeed, all stay at the same time and also with our lifestyle changes we would be unable to join in the many activities which we had both so enjoyed.

The other option, to move away, was more frightening but it would have many advantages. We could move down to the Chichester area, where we had a kick-start with our flat. Property prices were lower than where we were living at the time, so this would enable us to buy a reasonably sized property without a mortgage and start a new life. Bearing in mind the Surgeon's words, as this is what we had planned for our retirement we decided to go down this route with the added advantage that the sea air might help Luke.

Selling the house was not easy. It was a big house and although in a beautiful location, perfect for schools, it was probably out of the budget for families with young children. There were a few viewings but no buyers.

During this time, Luke started his course of radiotherapy. We were so blessed with the weather. Each morning seemed to be bright and sunny. We would get up at 6 a.m. have a cup of tea, and then do the slog to the Hospital for the radiotherapy. Usually home by 9.15, we enjoyed breakfast in the garden and Luke would then go back to bed and I off to work. How fortunate I was to be within ten minutes of my office as I was able to pop home at lunchtime and have a quick sandwich with him; my way of checking he was OK.

August Bank holiday was approaching when the Radiographer announced that there would be a break of four days during treatment, so we decided to take a quick holiday with some friends and go to Paris.

This was where we had spent our honeymoon and it was lovely to go back, especially as this was something, a few months previously, I would never have dreamt we would be able to do. We were a bit restricted as Luke was unable to walk far and he used a walking stick but we made the most of what we could and both of us returned feeling very refreshed.

Once again, God's hand was on us. No sooner had we got back from Paris than some dear friends, who had always liked our house, put in an offer and what a blessing that turned out to be.

The radiotherapy finished. The house sale was going through and we were able to go house hunting. We found a beautiful little chalet bungalow in Bosham near Chichester, but sadly were beaten in the race to buy it. The second house we found was in the vicinity of our flat. Doing our sums we were hoping to keep the flat on as our safety net, and rent it out to bring in some income. To enable us to buy this next property, however, meant we would have to sell the flat but thankfully, in hindsight, our offer was rejected. Then we had a stroke of luck –

was this also part of God's bigger plan for us?

We widened our search area and started looking at properties that were just out of our chosen area. One such property was on an estate with its own private beach. That particular house was a disappointment as it was completely unsuitable, however, as we drove through the estate, admiring the mixture of thatched cottages, beautiful old houses and well kept gardens we felt excited and decided that this location was definitely going on our search list. Then we spotted a 'For Sale' sign outside a mock Georgian house. We did an about turn and got a viewing, straight away.

The house had been on the market for several months. It was empty. The owner had died and the family were anxious to sell. Although still stuck in the seventies, bright orange kitchen, huge patterned carpets, avocado bathroom etc. it had great potential, and had everything we needed – four very large bedrooms, a large open plan entry hall/dining room, a sitting room arched into what was to become the study and a sunroom. Visually I could see the super, duper kitchen I planned. As we were cash buyers, we negotiated a good price, which enabled us to purchase the property without selling the flat, and two months later we moved in. At first we intended to live in our flat whilst we updated our new home but this proved to be too difficult as Luke was slow in the morning and by the time we got to the house we didn't have enough time to do all we intended. We had most of our furniture stored in various rooms in the house but slowly we unpacked it and after a few coats of paint here and there we started to occupy the rooms. We lived and cooked in the sitting room whilst the new kitchen was being put in and then at last it was completed and we could use it. It was splendid. A real joy to cook in and with enough room for us all to eat in, it soon became the hub of the house.

During this "well" time for Luke, we grew very close. We became real soul mates. Most days we would go for a gentle walk on the beach. We talked and shared a lot. Occasionally Luke would get depressed but somehow I managed to talk him round. The children came to stay and we spent quality time with them – something we had neglected to do when we were leading our busy lives. Friends came to stay and it was a very special time for us all. Then came the fire.

It had been a lovely Saturday evening. Luke and I sat in the conservatory, enjoying the last of the evening sun. As the sun disappeared we retired to the kitchen to do the washing up. Luke washed and I dried, as per usual. Half way through, we had a power cut. "Light some candles" Luke said "Much more romantic washing up by candle light". I did, placing two on the windowsill by the kitchen sink, so he could see what he was doing. He had lost the peripheral vision in his left eye but had few problems otherwise. Just as we were finishing the power returned.

"You go through to the sitting room, I'll just finish here" he said in his usual considerate manner.

Five minutes later, he called anxiously, "Pammi, I think you had better come here quickly".

I leapt out of my chair and ran to the kitchen, to find that the whole of the bottom of the curtains were on fire. Eventually with the help of the garden hose we extinguished the fire. What a mess. My beautiful kitchen had been destroyed. Everywhere was blackened if not burnt. The most frightening sound had been hearing the double-glazing popping. Shocked we stood and looked at each other.

"What do we do now?" I whispered.

"Telephone next door and ask Alan to come round," my still level-headed husband ordered me.

Alan, a well-respected Dentist and good friend was immediately with us.

"Call the fire brigade, so they can check that the fire is totally out and I will take some pictures for you for Insurance purposes".

I can still remember saying to the fireman "Please come and check the fire has gone out – you don't need to bring your fire engine!"

A gentle male voice at the other end of the phone reassured me "We will be there as quickly as we can Madam but I am afraid I do have to bring my fire engine."

Later, having ascertained that the fire hadn't spread, he reminded me of what I had said "You will find your comments quite humorous in about six month's time." He was so right.

We never knew exactly what had happened – whether Luke had not actually seen the candle to the left of him or whether it was one that had re-ignited after being blown out is anybody's guess but, whatever, the curtains had caught fire from the candle. It took several weeks before the house was back to normal again. Now, I rarely light candles but on the odd occasion when I do, they are never left unattended.

We were so blessed that we had this extra time together. Luke was almost always in denial that he wouldn't be around to reach retirement but occasionally it would hit him and we would cry together but we also laughed a great deal, making the most of awkward situations. Every morning on waking Luke would take my hand and would pray

> *"Thank you Lord for bringing us
> to the beginning of this new day".*

We joined a local Church and sometimes during the hymns we would sit and silently cry; in my case these were tears of joy and celebration that Luke was still with us.

We also had another great reason to celebrate. My son had become a born again Christian.

❋ ❋ ❋ ❋

5

ANDREW'S STORY

"Praise the Lord."

Just after we met when Luke and I started to go to Church regularly, as well as praying with gratitude for all the good things that had happened in my life, I prayed, as one does, for my children and their future. I had this vision of an oval shaped, walled garden: in the middle of this garden stood Jesus, in white flowing robes, with his arms open wide. Gathered in the folds of His arms were all my family with the exception of Andrew, who was hovering in the entrance to the garden. I continually prayed to God to bring Andrew into His fold. The Power of Prayer was once again answered.

✵ ✵ ✵ ✵

Part of the demands of my first husband in the Divorce agreement had been that he wanted custody of our son. Fortunately, the Judge saw fit to give us joint-custody but agreed to give care and control of our son to his father. As Andrew was at boarding school, to be able to continue his education and away from the hardship of us both rebuilding our lives it felt this was the right thing to do, although emotionally heartbreaking. It appeared to work. He came to me for some of his holidays but spent more times with his

Dad and new family. He secured a place at University in Scotland and decided to take a gap year. Six months later he was in a mess and it became apparent that the Divorce had unsettled him far more than we realised. His gap year was to be spent working with an Engineering company, learning the business. He rented a house with two other boys but in no time at all, through his own stupidity but also naivety he got himself in a complete mess. Unfortunately the company started to make redundancies and Andrew was laid off, at least this is what I was led to understand. The boys fell behind with their rent and got kicked out. Whether the other lads did not pay their bills or whether Andrew squandered the money, I don't know, but he was suddenly in debt. He got a job as a courier, borrowing a motorbike and with L-plates, delivered packages all over the country.

Communication was a phone call once a week. I assumed everything was fine until one evening, in 1988, just after we had moved into our Wisteria House, when he rang me. He was in tears.

"Mum, please help. I am in a right mess." He had no money, no food, and nowhere to stay. I was shocked. So wrapped up in my own busy life I realised I hadn't given much thought to what was happening to Andrew. I had adopted the formula that no news was good news.

The crunch had come when Andrew had driven his bike into the back of a car, which had braked suddenly in front of him. With no motorbike, there was no job. He had decided to go fishing and was caught fishing without a Licence. The downward spiral had hit rock bottom.

"Get on the first train here" I told him.

"I can't, I have no money, not even a bus fare."

With the aid of my credit card and a few phone calls we were eventually able to pick him up from our local station.

What a mess he was. Not only grubby with lanky hair, but with his black holey T-shirt and even holier jeans, he was not a pretty sight.

Luke suggested he had a bath, get changed and then he would take us out for a meal. He had nothing to change into – poor chap, he had just the clothes he stood up in.

The next few months were a real challenge. I wanted, with the help of his Dad, to pay off his debts. However, my ex dug in his heels and wouldn't agree. We were at loggerheads again. Stressed I went to see my GP, who was also a good friend, to seek his advice. He suggested we use a mediator to sort out the problems, as he could see that neither my ex or myself could be objective. As Luke was an Accountant and one step back from the emotional side, we agreed he might be the right person to decide the plan of action. As the advice had come from a sound source, my ex agreed.

Luke was insistent that if Andrew was going to live with us, he had to get a job and pay for his keep. He also suggested we give Andrew just enough money to get by on and use the rest to pay off his debts. I contacted all the companies he owed money to and to the Court for his fishing fine. Fortunately everyone, without exception, was sympathetic and, using Andrew's earnings, it was agreed to pay off as much as was possible as quickly as we could.

Andrew's first job was working on a vegetable stall on the Saturday market in town. This entailed getting there for 5 a.m. to unload the vegetables. Luke and I took it in turns to drive him there. Although he was earning very little it was a start on the road to recovery. He then procured a job in the kitchen of a local Pub – washing up, but the "big money" £120 cash a week, came from a builder who was happy to use my big son's strength on his building site. £30 of this went into housekeeping, which also covered his clothes. All the children had an allowance of £5 a week for telephone calls and anything over this they had to pay for them selves, this also applied to Andrew

£30 housekeeping seemed a lot but he was a big lad at 6' 4" and our food bill went up dramatically. He was given £20 in cash for incidentals and the balance of £70 went towards paying off his debts.

We had an interesting summer. Now and then he would disappear at weekends to spend time with an old school friend. Several times I had to pick him up, often at my insistence to make sure he got to work on time. Once Luke and I drove a few miles to pick him up and found him wondering around "stoned". It was frustrating. We would think he at last was growing up only to find he had slipped back and would disappear again. Usually he left a note but occasionally he would forget and without mobile phones we had to pray he would get in touch. However, by the end of the year when he was ready to go to University he had pretty well paid off all his debts and seemed to be settling.

❋ ❋ ❋ ❋

Going back to studying proved too much of a challenge for Andrew and he slipped back into some of his old ways, over-zealously enjoying University rather than working for his degree. He failed his first year.

However, he changed course and re-took the year, this time keeping his head above water, getting part-time jobs in Pubs and Burger bars and staying for the summer in Edinburgh with his then girlfriend. He finally emerged four years later with a 2-1.

At University he had made some good friends, with whom he kept in contact after he left. He found work with an Engineering company in Birmingham. The firm then recruited one of his closest friends, Dan, and together they rented a house in a grotty part of the town.

※ ※ ※ ※

It was the year after Luke's illness, when we were settled into our house by the sea that Andrew and Dan came to visit. Dan was a friendly and very likeable chap. He had become a born again Christian and was full of the joy of it all.

One evening, when we were sitting in the garden having chat over a relaxed drink, I told Dan of my vision of the walled garden with Christ in the middle.

"If only Andrew was more like you, and believed in God and what He can do," I said.

"He's not that far away" was Dan's reply.

It was just shortly after that when Andrew rang to say he was going to Ireland for the weekend to stay with Dan's parents and whilst they were there, they were going to hear some Preacher, he giggled as he told me.

It was no real surprise when he rang me the following week to report on the weekend.

"Don't laugh Mum, but I think I have just become a born-again Christian."

Laugh – no way, I was just so thrilled. Not quite so thrilled perhaps when he kept ringing me to ask if I had read my Bible today. Like a lot of people when they discover Christianity for the first time, he was full of it, in fact he was quite overpowering and drove his sisters to distraction.

"We do want to come and see you but if Andrew is there please tell him not to go on and on," they said.

However, from little seeds do big plants grow…

Andrew has never looked back. He married a lovely girl he met through his Church and I now have two beautiful granddaughters. Their commitment to their Church and lifestyle is amazing.

Praise the Lord

✻ ✻ ✻ ✻

WALKING ON EGGSHELLS

PART THREE

*Knock, and the door will
be opened to you*

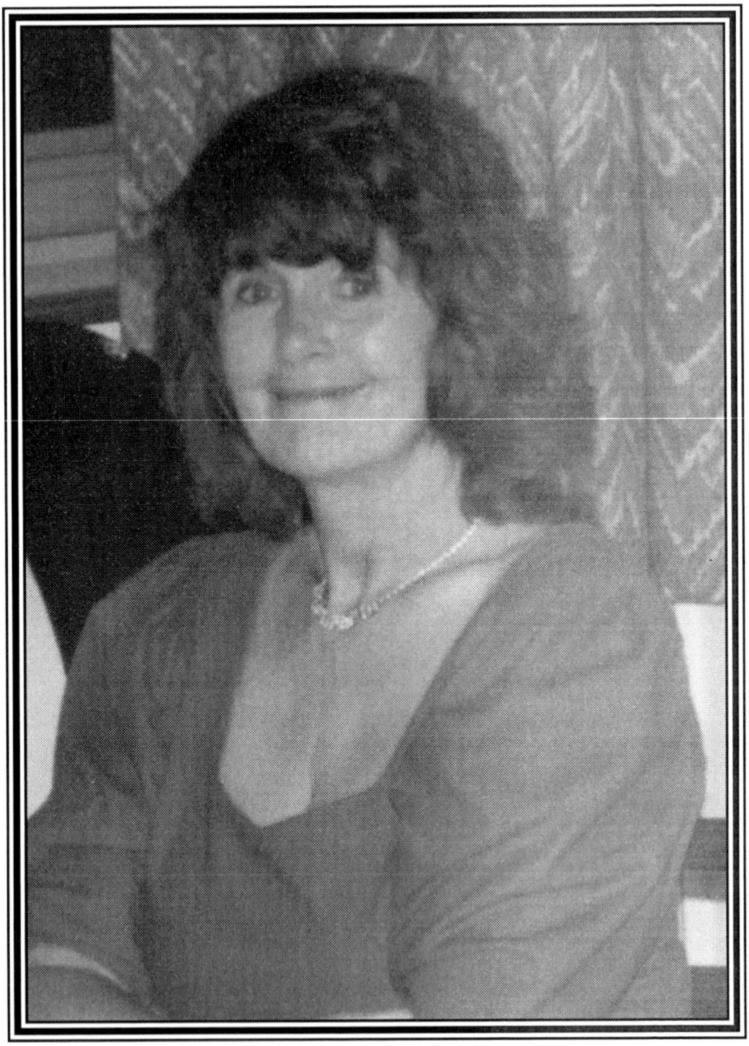

6

A TIME TO SAY GOODBYE

"A Very Special Time."

The radiotherapy was completed and we waited for the results. Luke was showing no signs of deterioration and all seemed to be going well, so it was a bit of a bombshell to be told that the radiotherapy hadn't worked. The residual tumour was still in situ, but the good news was that it didn't appear to have grown. A follow-up scan was scheduled for a month later. We were determined to enjoy ourselves as much as we could. Luke got himself a small job book-keeping, one day a week. This was mundane, compared to his high-powered jobs of the past, but at least it gave him a reason to get up in the morning and wearing a tie became a pleasure to him. He was still walking with the aid of a stick. He was continually on steroids which had made him balloon and unaccustomed to the extra weight, his balance was not good and on several occasions he toppled over.

I joined the Hospital Bank staff so that I could pick up jobs, which would fit in with Luke's schedule. We visited friends and friends visited us. We sat in the garden, we walked on the beach and we saw as much of the family as we could.

"I am getting too fat – you are feeding me too much" he

complained time and time again. He could never accept that the drugs were the problem. In fact, although when he started taking steroids he had shown a healthy appetite, this had dwindled but even with smaller, healthier meals he continued to put on weight.

The follow-up scan appointment seemed to come round very quickly. It was distressing news. The scans showed that the tumour was beginning to grow again. My vivid recollection of that time was hearing one of the staff muttering as she walked past me with Luke's X-rays saying "what a horror story". Was she talking about his X-rays, or what? I will never know but even though what she said was probably right, it was very insensitive. I have never forgotten this and it has held me in good stead, all these years later, keeping me aware of patient's feelings and sensitivities.

Chemotherapy was now the best option. At the beginning, the chemotherapy routine was relatively easy. We travelled back to our old hospital for the treatment, which gave us an opportunity to meet up with family and friends. The rest of the time I had the pleasure of issuing Luke with his pills. The anti-sickness drugs were great and apart from being tired he seemed to cope really well.

At the end of the course, this time we were delighted to be told that the scans showed that the new growth had been killed off. Now we could resume our almost normal life at least until the next lots of scans.

✳ ✳ ✳ ✳

A friend of my daughter, Grace, owned a flat near Malaga and offered it to us for a week. What an opportunity. Luke was well enough to travel and with the help of Grace and her boyfriend, Al, we booked the flights. Another obstacle was thrown at us, when the night before we were due to fly we had a phone call from the Agent to say that the Airline Company had gone out of business. However, with quick thinking the Agent had managed to book us on an alternative flight with a different airline. Two problems faced us – one, we would have to pay the airfare again and put in a claim for the fare already paid for and two, the flight left two hours earlier than planned. There was no dithering, our life together was limited and so we blew caution to the wind, paid up and went.

Little did I know that this was to be the start of another phase of this horrible disease.

Just before take-off, I noticed Luke had shut his eyes.

"Are you alright darling?" I asked anxiously.

"Sssh." he replied with his eyes still shut. Then he pointed to the floor.

"Bomb on board!" he exclaimed. Now it was my turn to do the "ssshing!"

You cannot imagine how I felt when there was an interruption to the taking-off procedures as the Cabin Crew announced that there was an unidentified case on board and that the baggage handlers were required to unload all the luggage for safety reasons. Had Luke had a premonition?

Three days later there was another incident. Luke had insisted that he had to go to a bank. Realising that he was likely to get into a difficult, stubborn mood, similar to the accusations regarding my over-feeding him, it was easier to go along with him. This difficult, stubborn mood was not all to do with his condition, as it was one of Luke's characteristics and something I had got used to over the years, but hey ho, it was never a big deal, so off we all went to the bank.

There was a queue to be served so rather than leave Luke standing, I suggested he sit in one of the comfortable settees until it was our turn. I joined the queue. Grace came in and sat beside him. After a few moments she got up and approached me screwing her finger to her head and whispered, "He is up to something Mum; I don't know what he is on about – you go and speak to him and I'll stand in the queue."

We swapped places. As I approached him, he looked up at me with a beautiful smile on his face, all signs of his moodiness gone,

"Pammi we have been invited out to drinks on Sunday."

"Really" I said, knowing that no-one, apart from Grace, had been near him whilst we had been waiting. Again I recognised that his brain was playing some kind of trick on him.

"Yes." he continued, "Edwardo DePlanto, he is the Manager here, has invited us to drinks at 11 o'clock on Sunday".

This was too spooky. I looked around, but there was no-one even remotely interested in us. Had such a person approached us I think I would have got on the next plane home. There are premonitions and premonitions but this was scary. I checked, there was no such Manager! Phew.

As the holiday went on I became aware that Luke was living in a dream like state. Sometimes he appeared perfectly normal and other times he acted in a most weird fashion.

However, I began to realise that in his 'dream like condition' his eyes looked different, almost as if he was sleep walking. It was much easier to go along with him when he was in this state, as he got agitated if you disagreed with him.

A few days later we were treated to another of his brains little pranks. We had had a perfectly normal day in Marbella admiring the boats and shops, stopping frequently for soft drinks; everything was very pleasant. As early evening approached we decided to have dinner at a bar restaurant on the beach, before returning to the apartment. We found some seats, settled down and the waiter brought the menus.

"I think I would like the garlic prawns," Grace smiled.

"Hmm they look good. I think I might have that also, followed by a pizza." I said watching the waiter taking some to the next table.

Suddenly Luke banged the table "One plate only." He said crossly.

Laughing I said "No Luke, you have got it wrong. One plate only was what we decided to do if we went back to that restaurant in Calahonda. You remember?" That particularly good restaurant had served enormous portions and we had been unable to finish everything, so had all decided that, should we return there, we would have one plate only".

Luke wasn't having any of it.

"One plate only." He said thumping the table with his fist and shouting.

"Ooops." I looked at my daughter and she nodded.

"OK, Luke we will all have one plate only." She said to him gently.

He gave her a broad smile. "Good, that's what we agreed."

No-one was going to argue.

On the way home he had another turn when he kept insisting we were driving in the wrong direction and that he wanted to get out and walk. This time we ignored him and as he and I were in the back of the two-door hire car, we felt he was safe, although being difficult.

He then adopted little habits, like refusing to leave the

apartment during the day, preferring to stay and read or fall asleep on a chair in the sitting room. We took it in shifts to sit with him, and got quite crafty at forgetting to take "things" to the pool so that he was never really left on his own. The time passed quickly and we were soon queuing for our return flights at the airport.

This again turned out to be an interesting experience. We managed to get a wheelchair for Luke and as we were waiting to board our flight, he informed me that Grace and Al had managed to get the last two seats on the plane before ours and would be well on their way home by now – very logical, except they were standing behind us as he spoke.

✳ ✳ ✳ ✳

On our return I talked to our G.P. about Luke's inability to know what was real and what was fictitious. He felt this needed to be reported to the Oncologist and quick as a flash another scan was ordered.

I think we were all a bit shocked to find that the tumour had started to grow again, presumably the pressure on the brain was causing these dream like states. Another course of chemotherapy was planned.

Luke resumed his bookkeeping work during the chemotherapy but within a few weeks I received phone calls from his boss. First it was to say that he had got lost in town whilst going to the bank and then they said he appeared to be day- dreaming in front of the computer but not actually doing any work. It was suggested that he have a break until his chemotherapy was finished – he never returned to his job.

By now he was showing definite signs of deterioration. We battled on together, making the most of each day and night. We were still sharing the same bed but Luke was getting more and more restless. The doctors had upped his dose of steroids; he gained more weight and often could not sleep. Eventually he asked me if he could move into the single bed in the spare room, as he felt he would feel safer being next to a wall and able to grip the side of the bed when he turned over. This seemed logical but sad. His dream like state had disappeared and he was quite logical for a while.

Then one night he got stuck in the bath. It was so funny that we both had tears falling down our cheeks as we tried to work out how to get him out of the bath. He suggested I just got blankets and he would stay there for the night but finally with lots of determination we got him out. That was the last bath he had.

Even having a shower was no mean fete but we managed.

✳ ✳ ✳ ✳

It was a hard winter and there was a 'flu epidemic', everyone was being advised to have a 'flu jab, so I rang our GP surgery and asked if Luke should have one. Because he was on chemotherapy, my GP agreed to do a house visit and give him a jab. Wow did the ball start rolling after his visit.

The Doctor spent a little time with me after he had seen Luke, asking questions about his treatment and his present condition. Although registered with this new GP, because we were having treatment out of the area we had never actually met him but what a clever man he was. Very tactfully, he suggested that maybe his District Nurse should look in and see if she could be of help.

My immediate reaction was "No, thank you". We were doing fine on our own and I wanted to nurse him myself as long as I could.

However, the Doctor was very persuasive and convinced me that, whilst they had no intention of interfering, there were areas where they might be able to make it easier for us both.

The next day District Nurse Chris rolled up. She was amazing and I liked her immediately.

"First, let me get you some help with showering him, he is a big man and you don't want him slipping do you?" Put that way, of course, I was pleased to have some help. She drew up a plan and suddenly I had help two days a week with showering Luke. Luke couldn't believe his luck. The 'help' with the shower turned out to be in the form of a young and very pretty nurse. At first he was very worried, "We can't afford it," he kept saying. It took a while for him to realise that this was part of the NHS service, something for which I will be eternally grateful. We had the most superb care from brilliant nurses to our very compassionate GP. They all became friends and we looked forward to their visits.

Nurse Chris arranged for an occupational therapist to come and see us and once again, I made a new friend. Grab handles were arranged for the shower and a handrail for the stairs.

❋ ❋ ❋ ❋

Luke was beginning to get very moody. We had always been a very tactile couple, holding hands and hugging in public, our love for each other shining out of every corner. Suddenly he didn't want to hold my hand any more and was becoming quite aggressive and nasty. It was soul destroying, even though I knew it was part of his condition, I didn't want to remember him like this.

In November we made our last trip to our old house. Luke was finding it harder to get around. The friends who had bought our house had made us feel so welcome every time we went back to our old town and we had stayed with them many times but I think we all knew, although never actually said so, that it was going to be the last time. On that occasion they gave us our old room, invited our many friends in for supper and just made us feel so welcome.

Luke was slipping in and out of his "moods" and they could see a great deterioration in him. Walking the dogs with my friends I remarked,

"I wish Luke would pass away whilst I can still remember how loving he has always been. I am finding it difficult to accept this change in him and I don't want to remember him as being vile to me."

Meantime, I kept praying for the old Luke to return.

Again, the Lord listened to me

and just shortly after this Luke returned to his usual loving self and stayed that way until he died, however, with the return to my loving man, came also the return of his dream like state.

By now his mobility was getting worse and Nurse Chris suggested we convert our study into a "day room" so that Luke could have a sleep during the day without climbing the stairs. She arranged for a hospital bed to be delivered. Within two weeks of it being delivered, Luke was sleeping downstairs. It was horrible being apart but at least I was able to get some sleep. My friend Sue, the OT, arranged for us to borrow a two way baby alarm, which was great as Luke could call me if he needed me and I could talk to him over the system. Just after we had it installed, I went down one morning to be greeted with another of his fantasies -
"Pammi we have to arrange a meeting."

"What would you like me to put on the Agenda?" I asked.

"Snoring." Luke grinned. "We must synchronise our snoring."

With his awkward shape affecting his balance, Luke had a few tumbles and on one such occasion fell out of bed.

Nurse Chris advised me to ring the ambulance service if it happened again as I couldn't lift him. She also arranged for cot sides – just in case. I did call the ambulance twice during that time, but then the cot sides went up. Looking back I could see the pattern – every step 'just in case' was a 'final' step towards the end for my poor Luke.

We were delegated a male Nurse, Sean. Sean was very clever; every day he asked me how I wanted to play it, in what order, time etc. I knew he was really the one in control but he handled us both so well it was a joy to have him in the house. We settled into a good routine, although I didn't sleep very well. It was like having a small baby again, when you seem to be constantly on the alert. Sometimes, Luke would call out at 2 a.m. for a glass of water, or just call out "Pammi are you there". It never bothered me, as I was more than happy to be there for him, but I did get tired. Still we adopted a routine that seemed to work well.

At 7 a.m. I would make a cup of tea for us both and then climb into bed with him. This was most uncomfortable. The bed was only designed for one although it could take up to 24stones in weight. So I had one buttock in bed next to Luke and one balancing on the windowsill. It was worth it just to have that special cuddle each morning.

About 8.30 a.m. I would give Luke his porridge – he was still able to eat by himself. We would then be ready for the bed bath, which Sean and I did together at 9.30 a.m. Luke's legs were very weak and although we managed to use a wheelchair to get him to the loo, showering was now no longer an option.

This routine was good for a few weeks but slowly and surely Luke was getting worse. A sling was installed beside his bed "just in case" along with a wheelchair/commode. What a nightmare that turned out to be. He had a catheter inserted and then was given suppositories once a day when Sean and I could operate the sling together to get him from the bed to the commode. Poor Luke. Fortunately dignity didn't come into it as he was unaware, a lot of the time, as to what was happening to him.

My daughters took it in turn to come down for the weekend. This was wonderful. When Grace came she took charge of Luke, giving me time to have a bath and relax a little. He was now in and out of sleep the whole time. But the minute he moved, she was out of her chair and couldn't do enough for him. Susie worked the other way and looked after me – cooking and taking over the household chores.

Luke and I had the saddest but funniest of conversations. One day as I brought him lunch, he asked me if I could see the giraffes and lions in the garden. Without thinking I said, "Oh darling we are in Bognor not in Africa." His expression changed from happy to immediate sadness, as I kicked myself for not remembering. After that I got used to seeing lions, tigers and giraffes in my garden, as I shared his joy at what he was seeing. After that we spent many times sitting together – he in his big comfortable hospital bed and me in an armchair beside him, holding hands and looking at the elephants in the garden. One time we were catapulted to Spain where we were in a bullring watching the matador and bulls.

Although obviously this was a very sad time, it wasn't without its joy. As Nurse Chris said one day, "I would just die to have someone look at me the way he looks at you. He loves you so much." He did and I so felt it.

❋ ❋ ❋ ❋

Christmas was approaching. I tried to persuade Luke's sons to come and see him but somehow, the seriousness of the situation seemed to escape them. Before he was totally confined to bed I overheard Luke talking to one of his sons about Christmas. It became apparent that his son was going off to the country for Christmas, despite our asking him to come and spend it with us. "Don't worry," said Luke "We are going to Scotland for Christmas and will probably stay there for New Year."

"What," I exclaimed. This had to stop now.

I managed to get to the phone without disturbing Luke and tried to explain to his son that we were going nowhere and, that as this would probably be his father's last Christmas, I felt it would be more appropriate that he should come to us. I don't think he believed me. I think probably his father had sounded too convincing. This was part of the problem, there were moments when he seemed perfectly normal and rational and we could have a good conversation as if nothing was wrong. Other times, we were in 'fantasy land'.

In a more coherent moment, Luke told me that he knew he was ill, although he still hoped to fight it. He had refused to accept that there was anything wrong with him that couldn't be cured so this was a revelation in itself. He said his main concern was for me. How I was going to cope without him? I wondered too but didn't say so.

My family came down for Christmas and my good friends

came for New Year. We all mucked in and made it a memorable Christmas.

Luke loved Christmas carols and so I arranged for some of the new friends we had made through church, including our Vicar and his wife, to come in one evening for some mulled wine, mince pies and a singsong. Luke sat up in his cot-bed and sang along with all the carols. Sadly the next day when I remarked how lovely it had been to have everyone singing carols, he couldn't remember.

"Were they here?" he said. This was how it now was for the next four weeks.

He slept more and more but when he was awake very often he was in his dream world. It was just as well in some ways, as he wouldn't have coped with the indignity of having every small detail now attended to for him. He had to be spoon-fed for all his meals and the baby cup with a lid on "just in case" came into its own. It was becoming a full twenty-four hour a day nursing job.

We had the backing of the local Hospice. After an initial interview, it was agreed that I could nurse him myself at home for as long as I felt able but that they were there for backup if I needed it.

A couple of times, I used their "sitting service" so I could go shopping but my mind was never away from his bedside and I was always glad to get back to him.

My home Hospice nurse, became a friend and counsellor. We often sat and cried together over a cup of tea in my kitchen, just as Nurse Chris and I did.

Luke's sons finally came to see him and I was very sad to see how shocked they were. They didn't stay but were back two weeks later for the funeral.

It was a Friday afternoon when Luke suddenly complained of neck ache. At no time had he complained of any pain in the preceding 17 months, apart from backache from the sling, and I could see by the look on his face that this was serious. I rang Nurse Chris and that evening a syringe driver was set up for me to administer morphine to him. The twilight nurses came in at bedtime to check on him. He was comfortable again. The next day although he acknowledged me with a weak smile, he was slipping away and I knew it. I couldn't bear it. I didn't want him to suffer any more, especially not for me. I needed to reassure him that I would be alright.

"Let yourself go, my darling. I will be alright. I have the children to look after me. Please don't put yourself through any more agony. The only thing I ask is that when you get to Heaven, you wait for me – no flirting." I am still convinced I saw a small smile circle his mouth.

That evening Grace persuaded me to get some sleep but I cried long into the night.

❄ ❄ ❄ ❄

The Sunday Telegraph Magazine ran a page on "Lifestyle". Inspired by some of the articles I read, I had written to the Journalist who ran the column telling her about our change of lifestyle, since Luke's illness. I didn't hear anything until just before Christmas when she rang me and said she would like to follow up my story. The first thing she wanted to do was to get some photographs of Luke and me together. I told her it was a bit too late but she felt it would still be of interest and arranged for a photographer to visit. This visit was arranged for Sunday, January 26th 1997.

At 2 a.m. on the morning of Sunday January 26th 2007,

Luke called out "Pammi." I was downstairs in a shot. Had I dreamt it? I didn't know but he seemed peaceful. I took his hand and settled in the chair beside him. Around 6 a.m. his breathing changed and I could hear his chest "rattling". Chris had talked me through all this and I was prepared.

Several times in the next three hours, I thought he had breathed his last long breath. Finally, at about 9.30 a.m. Luke passed away. I sat holding his hand and praying, thanking God that he had not been in pain when he died. I sat with him for some time then went and woke Grace.

After the undertakers had removed his body, Grace suddenly remembered – the photographer – he was on his way down to take photographs. She tried to contact him on his mobile but it was switched off. He was arriving at Bognor Station in about 30 minutes. Well, as they say, the show must go on and certainly that is what Luke would have wanted.

✽ ✽ ✽ ✽

Printed in the Sunday Telegraph a few weeks later was a very nice story with a picture of Grace, myself and the dogs on the beach. Luke would have been very proud.

✽ ✽ ✽ ✽

"I would die to have someone look at me the way he looks at you."

Many, many times I have remembered those words that Nurse Chris said to me, and many times I have thought how fortunate I was – that was

a very special time

and I was so privileged to be able to spend it with him. God gave me so much strength to cope with his illness that through the experience my faith and belief in God has got stronger and stronger.

❋ ❋ ❋ ❋

7

AMAZING GRACE

"Lead me Heavenly Father."

She was a beautiful child, always smiling and happy. As a toddler everyone adored her. She was my little angel. In her teens we had few scraps. We became friends through laughter and tears, as we shared our fun and mistakes. She helped me through difficult times; I felt so lucky to be so close to my daughter.

Grace went through University, coming out with a 2-1. I was so proud. She was very single minded and had incredible drive. She knew what she wanted and boy did she go for it. So, after working in PR for a year, it was no surprise when she suddenly announced that she wanted to be a Fashion Writer and was going to quit PR to work for a newspaper on work experience, learn the ropes and get known. When she left University she had been drawn to PR work in the Fashion Industry. She didn't enjoy working in a PR office, but it gave her time to decide into which area of fashion she should set her sites. With her mind set, this change of direction was exactly right for her. At the end of three months work experience, with one of the main tabloid newspapers, she was offered a permanent job as a Stylist. This she did, and enjoyed, and a few years later we were all so happy when she was head hunted by another well known tabloid newspaper's Magazine to become their Fashion Editor.

Luke and I had made several trips to London, occasionally staying with her in her rented flat, but with her new high-powered job it was time to start looking for a place of her own. She had spent a lot of time travelling to see us in Chichester and continued to come and see me after Luke died but it was obvious that she needed a home in London. We talked it through and I offered to help get her feet on the ladder. She fell in love with the first flat that she viewed. It was a typical London Victorian dwelling, on a busy main road, in an up and coming part of South London. It was 15 minutes walk to the tube station, but there was a bus stop right outside her building. The first floor flat had large airy rooms, a lounge overlooking a small courtyard, two double bedrooms and a large kitchen. It was perfect and so, as nothing else we looked at came even near, that was it.

Grace completely redecorated the flat in her own unique style, apart from one room in which I was allowed a say. I shall never forget her first day there. I arrived about 11 a.m. with breakfast. We sat around the large pine table, in her bright, sunny kitchen and ate bacon and eggs. It was a beautiful day. As we sat and took in the whole ambience, the sun shone and through the open window, we could hear birds singing. To our delight, that evening, from her bedroom window at the back of the house, we could hear a gospel choir singing Amazing Grace. It *was* amazing and I felt we were so blessed.

In Grace's first year in her flat, I went up many times. Mostly we went on shopping trips to furnish the flat. Lovely walks through Camden Market on a Sunday morning finding bits and pieces that Grace chose for the flat. Occasionally we would do a show. It didn't take her long to settle in and I was always pleased to hear of her triumphs and her disasters in her weekly phone calls.

As the first Christmas approached without Luke, we took ourselves off to Washington for a four-day shopping trip. That was fun and very exciting. I had always wanted to go to America; it was not a disappointment. The following summer my brother, Robin, joined us as we went off to Florida for a week. It was a fantastic holiday; very relaxed. We were a successful combination, as fortunately we all liked doing the same things. Grace and Robin got on very well so we all had an easy relationship with one another, despite the age differences. The following year we holidayed in Majorca and again had a great time. Grace was well settled in London. We kept in touch by phone and regularly met up for lunch or dinner, it was a comfortable time. We weren't intruding in each others lives, just enjoying sharing our experiences, much as I was doing with my other daughter and son.

Tuscany sounded nice and so, with Robin, we decided to book another holiday in the summer. However, with an extra week of holiday to take before the end of the financial year, I suggested to Grace that we squeeze in a visit to Scotland to see my aged Aunt.

Grace had just started a relationship with a new boy called Dirk, but was still keen to come with me to Scotland and visit my aged Aunt. Grace had had quite a few relationships over the years, all of them lovely young men, so I was looking forward to meeting him.

We had a good week in Scotland, but I sensed things were different this time as Grace spent many hours on the phone, unusual for her, but exciting and I was very pleased when

Dirk offered to pick us up from the train station on our return. I abandoned my idea of staying overnight with Grace in London, en route for Chichester, but looked forward to meeting Dirk, hopefully over a cup of tea and a bit of a chat. It was a bit of shock to find that Dirk had other plans, which certainly didn't include a cup of tea, or Mum. We were picked up, and I was hustled quickly to my station and left to my own devices. At first I was upset, not because of the quickness of my "put upon exit" but because for some reason Dirk decided to completely ignore me, making no eye contact, no chat and in fact I might just as well have not been there.

Young love, I thought, trying not to feel hurt. The one thing I had learnt from my mother was not to criticize your children's partners. So for the next few weeks whilst Grace sang his praises and was obviously very much in love, I enjoyed her confidences and bit my tongue.

The holiday in Tuscany was looming. The plan was for Grace and I to spend three days in Florence, culture vulturing, after which we were being joined by my brother and heading for a villa in the Tuscany hillside. With the success of our previous holidays, I was really looking forward to it.

About a week before we were due to leave my brother rang to ask if he could bring his gay partner with him. Although a bit hesitant, I couldn't really say no. Of course, it would be OK after all Grace and I could go off and do girly things together, I thought. The apartment was certainly big enough with three double bedrooms so it was arranged. A couple of days, prior to leaving, Grace rang.

"Mum would it be alright if I asked Dirk to join us, when we go to the villa?"

My heart sank. She sounded so bubbly; I tried to say no but then I thought of how miserable she would be, especially when she added that if he didn't come with us he was off to some other holiday destination and who knows what might have happened. So I succumbed.

The first few days with Grace in Italy were fine and we caught up with my brother and his partner and drove to the villa. From that moment, the whole holiday became a farce, with missing passports, baggage arriving with us at the villa, which didn't belong to us, food poisoning and temper tantrums. Dirk pretty well ignored me for most of the time except when we were in restaurants. It was easier to avoid sitting next to him than to try and have a conversation with him. It got to the stage that if Dirk and Grace were alone by the pool, I sat at the other end as I did not feel welcome. It was a dreadful holiday but a few days after we arrived home, when Grace rang to thank me for being so nice on holiday and saying that she had just had the best holiday ever – I realised that I must be a jolly good actress, as for me, it really had been the holiday from hell.

We were also becoming less close. Grace was finding it more difficult to meet up for lunch and any suggestion that I come up and stay was being met with resistance. Slowly, I realised that I was being pushed out but if she was happy that was all that mattered and I got on with my own life.

A few months later, Grace rang to say she was thrilled to bits as Dirk had asked her to move in with him. She was a bit cross when she didn't get an immediate response of 'yippee' from me but I hadn't got my actress's hat on. However, I managed to say

"Darling, if that's what you want, of course, I am pleased for you".

As time moved on it was obvious that we would have to do something with the flat. After Grace moved in with Dirk, she let the flat out to a friend but this wasn't working particularly well and finally Dirk suggested that they sell it.

I would like to draw a veil over the next year or so. My relationship with Grace was practically non-existent. She asked me only to ring in the morning before she went to work and those conversations were stilted and usually one-sided.

I was hurting a lot. I saw little of Grace, apart from a very occasional lunch, but those appointments, which is exactly what they were, were few and far between. When she rang to tell me that Dirk had proposed, I did put on my actor's hat but I had huge misgivings – all my instincts said how wrong he was for her but I could not interfere. I was asked not to be involved in the wedding plans apart from helping financially. Can you imagine how heartbreaking it was not to be allowed to help my daughter choose her dress and all the other little things that go with mother of the bride weddings, but at least I was being asked to the wedding. Fortunately Suzie was more co-operative and we managed a day bridesmaid shopping.

Grace had always loved Cornwall and so I wasn't surprised when they told me this was where they planned to marry. They had taken over a large sea-facing house in

Cornwall for the event and also for the week following, as Dirk's family from abroad were coming over. That was when I probably made one of the biggest mistakes, certainly in Grace's eyes, which I have ever made.

Over the phone at some stage, Grace had told me that she hoped Dirk's father was coming to the wedding. He was single and gorgeous and "you will love him Mum," she said. I loved them all. They were lovely, lovely people and I am afraid I took Grace literally and fell for this gorgeous man – Rod, – Dirk's father.

The wedding day was strange. It was wonderful being with all of my family and the few friends that I had been allowed to invite but there was still this distance between Grace and I. She seemed happy and that is all a mother ever wants to know so I tried to relax and enjoy the day.

Rod was charming. A real lady-killer and I fell for him, hook, line and sinker.

During that week, I had just such a good time. We were in a group most of the time but it was exciting.

We, being myself and a friend plus Dirk's family, took over the big house for the week, whilst Grace and Dirk rented a little cottage in the grounds. Most days the family went out exploring the countryside but we all got together in the evening taking it in turns to cook for the 14 or so people. Now and then they stayed and enjoyed being on the estate. It was on one of those days that Rod made his first move. Sitting in a large rocking chair in the old kitchen he said "I am going to have a cuddle with you before this week's out." Shivers shot up and down my spine. For some reason I was scared and I avoided opportunities where we might have been alone. Even when he walked me to "my room" one evening, I was quick to make sure I had the dogs with me, hastily kissed him good night, went in and locked the door. It was only after he had gone and I had returned to Chichester that I thought, "fool". I had wasted such an opportunity. It was the first time, since Luke's death, that I had looked at another man and felt real emotion. Oh I had been out with a few chaps and even had a brief relationship with one but in that case we both knew it was only a fling. However, this was different, so when Rod rang me and suggested I meet him in London for dinner, I jumped at the chance. He was staying in Grace and Dirk's flat with his daughter and other members of the family, whilst the honeymoon couple were abroad, so we arranged to meet there.

It was the first day of Wimbledon Tennis fortnight and I had been fortunate enough to get tickets, but despite leaving in the middle of a match, I was still ten minutes late. As I approached the road near the flat, I saw him standing on the corner looking for me. I melted.

During the meal he told me that the rest of the family had gone away for the night and we were going to be alone. I was so scared but so excited at the prospect of what might be ahead of me. It was a magical evening and being held in this gorgeous man's arms was just so wonderful.

Rod returned to his home in New Zealand the next day and my heart was broken but then I had a letter from him, it sounded as if it was special for him too. We corresponded and spoke on the phone for the next few months and then I made the momentous decision to go out to New Zealand for a holiday on my own.

Although I had planned to see something of the Island, once I was back in Rod's company, I didn't want to go anywhere. He was everything I could possibly want and I was falling in love all over again. Grace and Dirk seemed happy that I should be out there with him and Rod took me to meet the rest of his family. I particularly liked his sister-in-law, Julie, she was fun to be with and it was good to have a girlfriend out there. He also had another friend, a girl called Teresa, whom I couldn't take to, not surprising, as I found out later that she had considered herself to be Rod's girlfriend.

I suppose I didn't think anything of the fact that she rang most days but apart from a lunch out with the family, she didn't join us at any time during my three week stay and I had no reason to think there was anything going on there. Julie informed me that the family all thought I was the right person for Rod and that was all I really wanted to hear.

Rod then had a rather strange telephone call. It was towards the end of my last week. It was Teresa and she had decided she wanted to come and spend the weekend with him, to watch the rugby, so she said. Rod didn't know what to say, apparently, this was a very unusual thing for her to do, I was mystified. We had been to lunch at Theresas but I certainly didn't get the impression that they were more than friends but still a doubt was beginning to form in my mind – was there more to Theresa than first thought?

It was Thursday night, we were having dinner at Julie's house and after a few drinks too many, decided to stay the night. Rod mentioned the fact that Theresa was intending to join us for the weekend and I can remember to this day Julie's comment "that could mean big trouble". A shiver passed through me leaving me with an impending sense of doom. That night I prayed like I have never prayed before, "please God, don't let her come and spoil my last weekend with Rod and the happiness we have had."

The next morning we returned to Rod's house where he picked up a message on the answer phone from Teresa's brother. Teresa had been taken into hospital with suspected pneumonia. I was sure my prayers had not been answered in this way but it had happened, Teresa would not be coming that weekend.

We decided that I should return to England as planned, whilst we both sorted out our feelings. I would go out again later in the year for a trial run to see if this was the "real" thing before committing myself to a move to New Zealand.

A few weeks after I got home, Rod gave me the devastating news that Teresa had been diagnosed as having cancer. It was all a bit of a shock but I understood that Rod was a good friend and going to have to be available for her to take her for treatments etc.

About eight months later she was in good remission. They thought the cancer was pretty well gone and it seemed like a good opportunity for me to return to New Zealand and for Rod and I to decide what sort of future, if any, we had. Now was a good time for Rod to tell Teresa why I was coming back. A week before I was due to leave, I had a phone call from Julie. "We think that you should not go to Rod's place. Come and stay with us at our beach house and Rod can join us there. Teresa is going to make trouble. She is really upset and she can be vicious. I suggested Julie speak to Rod and ask him what he wanted me to do. He wanted me to go to his home as planned. "Teresa won't cause a problem. I have told her and I will speak to her again," was his answer.

As the plane touched down at the small internal airport

I could see this lovely man waiting outside for me. Judging by the racing of my pulse, I certainly hadn't had a change of heart. As I ran into his arms and he held me tightly, I felt my heart would burst with happiness. On the way to his house, he stopped off to buy some fish and I felt my stomach tightening when I heard him ask for three pieces of fish but I felt sure that he would have sorted things out. How wrong can you be!

We were sitting on the deck having a quiet drink, taking in the late afternoon sunshine, listening to the birds, after having had a lovely cuddle when a car drove up the long path. It was Teresa. I was told that this was all completely out of character for her, as she never normally saw him during the week! She came in, smiled and said to Rod, "I'll get the supper on then". I don't know which was worse, the shock of her sudden arrival or the shock of her appearance.

She looked paler, thinner and was wearing a black turban on her head, a reminder that, although she was in remission, she had been seriously ill. She bustled about in the open plan kitchen refusing my offer of help but involving Rod when she could. Dinner was served on our laps in front of the TV. This was not quite what I had expected as, in the past, Rod and I had eaten dinner out on his deck, talking and listening to music every evening until well into the night but here we were in front of the TV and little conversation. Rod kept drinking and drinking until about 8.30 p.m. when he got up out of his chair, looked at us both and said, "Well, girls I am off to bed, goodnight" and disappeared. I was stunned.

Teresa and I talked a little and I can remember looking at the clock, thinking "is she never going to go home' when, just as suddenly, she got up and said "Right I am off to bed too." and disappeared after him.

Shocked, I staggered to my hut in the garden. In New

Zealand a lot of houses have huts in the garden, which are converted into living accommodation. Although dated, my hut was lovely. It was warm and it had shower, loo and kitchen so it was very acceptable living accommodation. This is where I had stayed the first time I had visited Rod and he had stayed there with me too, only using the main house for cooking and sitting on the deck. It was our little love nest, but not tonight.

I could hear them arguing but that was of no help as I cried myself to sleep. For the next two days, I never saw Rod on his own. Everywhere I turned, Teresa was there. Finally I thought enough is enough and gave him an ultimatum – she goes or I go – even that had to be done surreptitiously, with a piece of paper slipped into his hand. She went. We tried to pick up the pieces but it was too late. The damage was done and I started to see him in a different light.

I found out later that when he told her my real reason for coming to NZ the second time, she had gone off the deep end. Obviously there had been far more to their relationship, certainly in her eyes, than I had been led to believe.

A letter arrived two days later, in which she declared the end of their friendship.

He rang up all the family, and judging by the comments, it appeared that everyone was relieved and welcomed me with open arms. That night Theresa rang to find out if he had got the letter. The next day she rang, and the next and the next. It was obvious she was not going to let go that easily.

Despite misgivings, having made the long journey, I decided to stay my full three weeks and make the most of it. It is a beautiful country and so we did quite a bit of sightseeing, but there was a definite change in our relationship. I saw a lot of Julie who was becoming a true friend. Then he had the phone call that was to completely change our lives. Theresa had to see him, today, now. For the first time, we exchanged angry words. Mine along something like "If you keep jumping to her every command we will never be free," and he defending their 14 year friendship. I rang Julie who suggested we go out for lunch, whilst he went to see Theresa. To save extra car journeys, I arranged to meet Rod in the supermarket later in the afternoon. I was shocked when I met him, it was obvious he had been crying and although he did his best to hide it, something traumatic had happened. That evening he consumed double the amount of alcohol, finally becoming verbally aggressive, accusing me of all manner of things. It was time to go. The next morning I asked him to run me into town so I could change my ticket and leave on an earlier plane.

When he finally waved me goodbye at the airport, I felt sad as if I was leaving under a cloud. This is the bit where he was supposed to run after the plane saying he had made a mistake but, of course, this was real life.

In the meantime, things back home were not going so well for Dirk and Grace.

During my stay with Rod, we had had several funny phone calls when they both sounded a bit drunk "Go for it Mum", they encouraged me, but now back at home in the cold sober light of day, it was obvious things were not so jolly.

Grace started ringing me more regularly and we arranged to meet in London. Whilst I was overjoyed that we were getting together again, I could see something was not right, but she kept reassuring me that everything was fine. She didn't look ill but she had lost the sparkle that was Grace. I was worried.

And rightly so – it was not a total surprise, therefore, when I had a desperate phone call from her to say that Dirk had not come home one night. Re-assuring her that he had probably had too much to drink and stayed with some mates, my mother's instinct knew this was not the case. This happened several times more.

"Could he be seeing someone else?" I asked

"No, Mum, he would never do that to me," was her response.

But finally the truth came out when he confirmed that he was having an affair,

She was devastated. I offered help but she threw it back in my face.

"It's all your fault Mum, if you hadn't had an affair with his Dad, none of this would have happened." She believed this and I was absolutely heartbroken.

What a bastard to blame me for his inadequacies and how dare he break my daughter's heart.

The next few months were probably the most painful of my life. I loved my daughter so much and here I was being blamed for her destruction.

Now God works in mysterious ways and this was to be the proof of the pudding.

During this time of devastation, Grace took herself off to Australia to "find herself". She needed to get away. Susie, her sister, was the only person in whom she would confide and so although I had no direct contact with her, Susie kept me in the picture. Grace had gone to stay with a girlfriend in Australia whilst she sorted herself out and decide what to do with the rest of her life.

It was on one beautiful morning in Australia; the sun was shining, the flowers were blooming, when a great sense of peace pervaded her. God had come into her life, touching her gently – she was not only on the road to recovery but on to greater things and a huge witness to His presence.

8

GLORY GLORY HALLELUJAH

*During this traumatic time, we had
yet another witness to God's workings.*

Suzie and I had been sworn to secrecy as to Grace's whereabouts. She did not want anyone else to be told and we both respected her confidentiality.

About ten days after Grace's departure to Australia, I had a telephone call from Andrew.

"Mum, I have had a vision. Have you spoken to the girls this week?" My son has many visions and they all have some significance so I listened as he astounded me, "There is something wrong with one of the girls. I believe it is Grace. Someone is being adulterous and I think it is Dirk."

"Don't say things like that Andrew" I retorted, trying to hide my emotions.

"Mum, it was a real vision. Are you sure they are all right? I have tried ringing Grace but her mobile is switched off."

"I'll get in touch and let you know" I said and changed the subject.

He then said he was coming down to Chichester for a day with his job and he would pop in and see me.

I panicked. What was I going to do; I knew I wouldn't be

able to hide my sadness. I rang Suzie and told her.

"OK I will text Grace and ask her if we can let Andrew know what is going on."

A few hours later she rang to say that, yes I could tell Andrew but no-one else for the moment as, if Grace worked things out with Dirk then she didn't want anyone to know what had happened.

Later that week sitting in the kitchen, I told Andrew the story. He smiled.

"What are you smiling about?"

"Oh Mum, I just knew. God sent me a message and I knew."

I found out later that "the message" had come through to him on the previous Sunday when at the same time, Grace, in Australia had also experienced a "vision" which was that she must seek out her brother and speak to him. They had never been close and he was usually the last person she wanted to speak to but how things were about to change.

Grace returned from Australia and immediately contacted me.

"Mum can you make an appointment with our Solicitor I have decided to divorce Dirk and perhaps I could come to lunch".

Come to lunch! I was overjoyed.

The solemn little girl, who stood on my doorstep, had aged by 20 years. It was a shock to see this beautiful daughter of mine with all the sparkle gone from her.

We had lunch but I don't think either of us could eat anything. We hugged and cried but still there was this huge wall between us. She talked little about the past. Then she told me about her trip to Australia. Towards the end of her three weeks there she had suddenly been aware of the birds, new growth in flower beds and the feeling of "something out there" had reached her. This was getting exciting. We now know that

this was the hand of God touching her

but at this stage she had still a long journey ahead of her.

"Don't get excited Mum," she said, "I am not ready to go to church but I do believe there is something out there."

Thinking quickly I remembered there was a "young" church in London where, if my memory served me correctly, was where the Alpha courses had started.

"Why don't you go on an Alpha course" I was even more excited but tried hard not to show it, knowing only too well what a turn off it can be when newly 'born again' Christians try to ram religion down your throat.

When she left that day I felt we might just have turned a corner.

Andrew said the same thing to Grace when she went to see him. They had never been close but this was a new beginning for them both. He answered her many questions and encouraged her to try an Alpha course.

She lived in London not too far from Holy Trinity Church in Brompton and she decided she would try the Alpha course.

She never looked back. There were many heartbreaks in between where she is today and then. Her divorce was painful but again HTB ran Divorce Courses and this was helpful to her.

Still our relationship was cool. Sure we talked to each other more frequently, she came to see me and I would meet her for lunch occasionally in London but still she believed that I had a lot to do with the reason for her marriage breakup.

Christmas 2002 was strange. Since Luke's death, Christmas had become something to dread. Everyone else in the world seemed to be happy but the sadness of being parted from Luke was always there and try as I might, the loneliness was still there. The fact that he had died just after Christmas was also meaningful to me. This particular Christmas I took Grace along with Andrew and his wife, Davina, away to an apartment in Norfolk where I hoped we were going to have a good time. Unfortunately, like previous Christmas's I became ill with chronic diarrhoea, which meant I was unable to partake in some of the activities and I felt quite debilitated. We got through the festive period but a cloud hung over us all and certainly I could still feel a certain amount of coldness towards me from my beloved daughter, although I do believe she tried very hard not to show it. On my return home it was necessary to see my GP as I was at my lowest. He was a lovely man. When his Practice had been short staffed I had helped out putting on my secretarial hat and got to know him and the staff quite well. I was also a very infrequent visitor to the Doctor and he knew there had to be something really wrong for me to be attending as a patient.

The diarrhoea cleared up and he jumped on my depression.

"I know its no good suggesting you take antidepressants but would you consider counselling?" He asked me kindly.

No way, I thought. Counselling is for wimps. So I struggled through the next couple of weeks. During this time Grace had rung me several times to see how I was doing. Andrew had also rung me but had added to my depression by telling me that he kept having a vision of me sitting alone in a rowing boat moving round and round in circles going nowhere. He was convinced I needed a new direction in my faith – new Church, new Christian friends, something that would take me from my present circumstance.

Then I had a phone call from Grace that was to change my life.

"Mum, HTB run a Bereavement Course. Why don't you come and do it. It's on a Monday evening for six weeks and you could stay here afterwards for the night."

I didn't need a second asking. This was my big chance to get back to being close to my daughter again, even if it meant sitting through some sort of counselling, but at least it was away from Chichester and no-one would know me. So I booked it.

For six Mondays I travelled up to London to do the Monday evening course, returning refreshed each Tuesday morning.

Grace and I didn't see as much of each other as I would have liked because usually by the time I got to her flat, it was straight to bed but it was a start.

The Bereavement Course was brilliant. Suddenly I wasn't alone in my grief. I met up with three girls from Africa who had lost their Dad. They were lovely girls and really took me under their wing. Another girl had lost her Mum and was struggling with her Dad's broken heart, my heart broke for her. There was a widow of ten years and a widow of two years we all had something in common and could open up without fear of reprisal.

I will never forget my first evening there. Our Counsellor introduced herself and told us that she had been running the courses for 15 years in London but that her home was in a village near Chichester!

When I told Andrew, he was excited. "Find out which church she goes to when she is at home down near you, if it is as charismatic as HTB that could be the one for you," he said.

So after one of our sessions I asked her. She named a

church on the outskirts of Chichester. "Actually we are not home very often but when we do go down, that is where we go. It is excellent, give it a try."

Eventually, one Sunday morning, a little nervously, I went along to see what it was like. There were friends from the Theatre, the Hospice where I did voluntary work, and the tennis club. It was such a surprise. They made me feel so welcome and I had a very strong feeling that this was it – this was where I was meant to be. The first two hymns were two of my favourites and I felt already at home. But there were a few more God given surprises for me round the corner.

9

HOW GREAT THOU ART

"God Opens Many Doors."

Elated at finding this new church I began to reassess my life. Was this to be my new church? It was a good 20 minutes drive from where I was living. Perhaps I should move.

Not long after Luke died, I was thrilled when I found that some very dear friends were moving down to the coast and had bought a house only five minutes from me. It was like an anchor in a storm. They became even closer friends as we saw each other at least once a week, now I was considering moving away. In a dither I walked along the beach asking God to give me some answers.

It was Andrew who passed on God's message. He rang me with yet another of his extraordinary visions. "Mum, I have seen you in the rowing boat again but this time there is a lighthouse and a harbour. This has got to be of significance. Look for a lighthouse, that's what God wants you to do."

Well, for goodness sake, I live by the sea: of course there are going to be lighthouses.

"But how will I know which one." I asked, my seemingly crazy, son.

"You will know" was his confident answer.

About two weeks later I decided to venture back to the

new church and see what was going on. There was another warm greeting from friends. I settled into the service. The Vicar started his sermon. He talked about legal documents requiring two witnesses, just like we have two witnesses to God. The Bible and by word of mouth. He pointed to the cross beside the Bible, "the written word and now," he said, pointing to the window,

> *"I want you to imagine that candlestick on the windowsill is a lighthouse."*

I heard no more, the hairs on the back of my neck stood up, this was it; exactly what Andrew had said – I would know.

> *This was affirmation from God, I had found my church.*

Next, find a house not too far from the church and near enough my old friends to visit once a week.

When Luke and I were house hunting, we had looked at a town house on the edge of Chichester. It was in a lovely position but we had decided not to go with it as, being on three floors, it was bigger and more expensive than we wanted; plus the main room was the wrong shape to take my baby grand piano. I had never forgotten its position, its facilities and beautifully kept gardens. I knew there were some apartments near by so I decided to go and have another look. There were no for sale signs anywhere.

    Just as I was about to leave, a car drew up and an elderly gentleman asked if he could help me. Although there were no apartments up for sale, he gave me the name of the Estate Agents who usually dealt with the site sales and I rang them and asked for information.

"What a shame" said a very nice young lady "We have had one on our books but it has just gone, although they have not exchanged yet."

After a little bit of persuasion, (I offered to give them sole Agency to sell my house providing they would let me have a look at the apartment so I would know if it was definitely where I wanted to be) they agreed. It was a wet and windy day when I went to view, but the moment I walked inside I knew it was for me. Although I knew I couldn't have that particular flat, as the others were of similar design, I was prepared to sit and wait, renting somewhere if necessary, should my house sell quickly.

My house went on the market. We had lots of viewers and then an offer came in. I liked the couple. They were young, but as he was a partner in a professional company, I didn't envisage any problems with finance. However, one afternoon on their third visit they told me that their buyer was refusing to pay the full asking price for their property. Rather than lose the sale, I offered to drop my price to accommodate this and we shook hands on the deal.

I was even more ecstatic when the Agents rang to say an apartment had just come up for sale in my chosen area. I put in an offer, which would leave me quite comfortable. The owners went off to consider it and in the meantime someone else put in an offer. Now we were in a race and the price was going up and up. After a talk with my Agents, I decided to go to the top of my budget – after all, the flats were rarely on the market, it was exactly where I wanted to be, with its excellent facilities and nearness to church, it was perfect.

My offer was accepted and everything was set for an early exchange for both the flat and the sale of my house. The day before exchange, a day I will never forget, my buyers pulled out.

We often hear about broken chains, but I wonder how many broken hearts come from broken chains. Still convinced that it was God's plan for me to move near my new church, I sat down with the Agents to see how we could still purchase the apartment. These were days when it was easy to borrow money and so with two hefty, interest only, mortgages I went ahead with the purchase of the apartment. My brother said I was either very stupid or very clever – I was neither, I was just desperate. The mortgage brokers weren't afraid to lend the money as they had claim on two expensive properties. The house was back on the market but there was no real interest. A couple of low offers came in but I worked out that to reduce the price to what they were offering was the same as paying the interest only mortgage for 5 years and surely by that time I would have sold. So I hung on.

We were now into the quiet time and my only concern was keeping the house warm and free from burst pipes. The indoor pool which I had built after Luke's death, also needed to look sparkly at all times.

I moved into my apartment. It was lovely but the edge of the pleasure was taken off slightly by the worry of having to go over to the house every other day; then a friend who was a Renting Agent rang me and asked if I would consider renting my house as she had a prospective client. It seemed like a temporary option so we met up to talk it through. There would have been a good income, enough and more to cover one of the mortgages but when I read all the do's and don'ts of letting I decided against it. I also wanted the house to be available for viewing at all times as my priority was to sell it and as quickly as possible.

On 30th November I had a telephone call from a girl I had met in Church. They were due to move the next day as they had sold their house but she was in panic mode as she felt the house they were about to rent was too small and wondered if there was any possibility I would rent my house to them. My first reaction was to say no but then I stopped and considered all the advantages. Having someone in the house, looking after it over the Christmas and New Year period, negating the necessity for me to go there every other day was a good enough reason.

If I let the house through Agents it had to be a minimum let of six months and these people were unlikely to want it for that long. The only downside was when they admitted they could only afford to pay me a third of what the Agents had offered.

However, had God had a hand in this, helping us both? We agreed a compromise; for the very low rent, they would allow prospective viewers to look around and would keep the house tidy. There would also be a month's notice on either side. Renting it out for a couple of months or so seemed like a good idea. This was enhanced when in early January, Grace rang to say she was taking a two month sabbatical from work, going off to see the world, starting in Australia, where she would have some free time. What an opportunity to join her. My tenants were still looking for somewhere to buy but obviously quite settled in my property.

On my return, I was disappointed to find that there had been no interest at all in the property, so after discussion with the Agents I decided it was time to think it out again. My tenants had now been in my house for four and a half months, were obviously very comfortable but I was losing money by the day. It was agreed that I should ask my tenants to leave and then completely redecorate and remarket the property. My tenants indicated they might be interested in buying but no sensible offer was forthcoming and this was wasting time. I gave them 6 weeks notice. For once I was insistent we stayed with the deadline, even when they asked for another week. Thank goodness I did. They moved out on the 31st May and on the 1st June, before I started redecoration, I had a serious buyer.

I finally parted with my house on September 30th – a whole year after I had moved into my apartment. Financially in the end, I just about broke even but it was a decision I never regretted as

*God was about to open
many more doors.*

10

GOD WORKS IN MYSTERIOUS WAYS

The move to Chichester was one of the best things I have ever done. My relationship with Grace had changed for the better and things were looking up.

Grace's commitment to the Lord was becoming more and more. Through her church she started working with youngsters in Sunday school and then moved to helping an older group, eventually joining sessions reaching out to teenagers, in particular helping to get young girls off the street. She had always been resourceful so I wasn't surprised to hear that she had been using her knowledge of fashion to attract the girls, even showing them how to make a handbag out of a pair of old jeans.

"I want so much to help these girls, Mum. I want to write a magazine that, whilst still promoting the fun of being a teenager will have a more moral approach. I am appalled at the encouragement some of the teen magazines give to sex before marriage, sleeping around etc., how can the girls ever have respect for themselves?

"Pray about it for me. I need guidance as to where to start. I know God will tell me as to the timing and the where and when."

Then came a glorious opportunity to bring us even closer.

Grace had decided to take a two month sabbatical from her job and visit the southern regions of the world. Starting with a friend's wedding in New Zealand she then planned to go to Australia where she was to spend ten days before joining a friend to continue her trip.

"I shall have ten days on my own in Sydney Mum" she said.

"Why don't I fly out and join you" the words came out before I had even time to think it through.

"Why don't you?" I didn't need second asking.

The arrangements were made, flights booked and the day arrived. What excitement it was to arrive at Sydney Airport and hear a voice calling through the crowds "Mum!" There she was standing at the top of the slope where we were filtering through security. Grace had flown in from New Zealand. The flights arrived within minutes of each other, and some how she had spotted me. The tediousness of slow moving lines was ignored as we caught up with each other. Ever diligent, and as she was still employed as a fashion journalist, Grace had arranged to do some photo shoots whilst in Australia. Even this was fun as I was privileged to watch her work. Our hotel on Bondi Beach was in an ideal situation and she used this as a base for the models.

Unfortunately some of the shoots took longer than the couple of days she had put aside but we still managed to have beach time and most of all talking time.

We visited a local church on the Sunday and were made to feel most welcome. I watched in amazement at how easily Grace could talk and pray about the Lord to everyone and realised what a gift she had. We parted company at the end of her trip to Australia and she headed off for Indonesia and I left for New Zealand.

The first time I set foot in New Zealand I had loved it. There was something magical about the fresh air and the light – a real feel-good feeling. Walking from the International Terminal to the Domestic Terminal I felt as if I had arrived home.

I had made arrangements to stay with a friend for a few days and planned to visit the Bay of Islands. I had no intention of meeting Rod, but with the best will in the world I succumbed and we met up again for one more time. I am so glad we did because even though the magic was still there, I knew that it was time to move on. We parted friends and I now have treasured memories.

I had laid a ghost.

A few weeks after my return home, I had a phone call from Grace.

"I was going to tell you when I next see you but I can't wait, I am so excited. God has spoken to me and I now know what I have to do. You know I have always wanted to write a magazine for young girls, well now I know where God wants me to be… Cambodia. The young factory workers there need something and I can help."

After the shock of realising that Grace was leaving her high powered job to live in Cambodia and do mission through business, came the reality. First she was advised to go on a mission training course. She did her research and through her church was able to get this organised.

All her savings were needed to support her through this and she asked if she could come and live with me when she needed a home. They were infrequent visits but it was such a joy to have even a few days with her. The course was very successful and armed her with all the information she needed to prepare her for her new venture. She made a lot of friends and, in particular, one who had a lasting affect on her, Steve.

Eventually the time came for her to leave for Cambodia. We had a fabulous Christmas together with all the family. These days the sheer joy of having the whole of my family together is the greatest gift and we had a ball. Grace left, mid many tears but fortunately with good email and text contact we were able to follow her progress.

Many people had doubts as to whether she would ever get a licence to produce the magazine. We were constantly asking people to pray for her safety and for her magazine to become not just a reality but a success. I had joined a local Bible Study Group and a special prayer was always included for her. She braved many battles in a country notorious for its crime wave but finally obtained her licence.

The power of prayer was working,

so much so, that when she asked for us to pray for her to find the means to buy a car, so she could transport the magazine to the various factories etc., should we have been astonished to find that a donor had already set up a donation which would cover this? The magazine went from month to month financially. She employed local girls to run it – one of them an ex-prostitute – and each month they prayed that funds would come in, sufficient to carry them through to the next edition. There was great interest in the magazine, highlighted when Grace was invited out to lunch with the Deputy Prime Minister, who thanked her for all the work she was doing for the factory workers.

She managed to get home for occasional holidays and it was on one such occasion that I asked her if she had ever met any other young men or was remotely interested in meeting anyone again.

"Well, there is one Mum, whom I really did like. I only met him once but I don't think anything will happen as he lives in Africa, although I think that is where I want to go next."

It was on the next occasion when she was home, an Easter visit, that his name was mentioned again. "Steve and I have been communicating by email and he is going to be in London when I am here. I might suggest we meet, what do you think?"

Three days after they met I returned home to find her in floods of tears, 'ooops, I thought, "wrong decision" only to find these were tears of joy not sadness. Steve had written the most beautiful letter to her proclaiming his love. Even in these early days I could see a spark and wasn't at all surprised when she asked if I would mind if she spent some of her precious summer holiday in Africa rather than with me. "After all, how am I ever going to know whether he is the one if I don't spend some time with him." Her trip to Africa and later in the year his trip to Cambodia confirmed for them both that

this was the Lord's plan.

Planning Grace and Steve's wedding was no mean feat. With Steve in Africa and Grace in Cambodia there was a lot Mum could do and I was delighted. July brought torrential rainfalls and we were concerned. Grace wanted to keep the Wedding spiritual and simple. A church wedding in her spiritual church followed by afternoon tea in the garden, seemed the perfect solution but we had a few problems to overcome. Grace had been married before and, as yet, some church's were refusing to marry divorcees in church. However, we were delighted when Steve's father, a Methodist Minister agreed to marry them in the Methodist Church and then would follow a Blessing in Grace's Church. This was the perfect solution. They decided to do this over two days.

When she mentioned that she would really love to have the London Gospel Choir sing at their wedding, but it was beyond their means, I had the solution. This could be my wedding present to them. Now with the rains and the winds forecast, the tea in the garden looked doubtful. The good Lord had other ideas and we awoke on the day of the wedding to blue skies. We were so blessed with the weather as both days were glorious. It was a very emotional and joyous wedding and the garden tea party was a resounding success.

After a few weeks in Britain they finally left for their new adventure as missionaries in Africa.

Just before they left, Grace said to me, "I feel so blessed with you and Dad, Mum. You never tried to stand in my way, you just continued to give me your love and support in whatever I wanted to do even when I threw in my job."

> *God works in mysterious ways.*
> *I am sure He laid it on our hearts that*
> *she would make a success in whatever*
> *she did in His name.*

❋ ❋ ❋ ❋

During this time, Grace's dedication to the Lord also had a profound affect on my lifestyle. I had had one or two boyfriends, after my love affair with Rod, and indeed was in another relationship when Grace gave her life to the Lord.

Although Grace liked my partner, she wasn't happy that he was a non-believer and told me quite bluntly I shouldn't be sleeping with him –

> *"Do not be yoked
> together with unbelievers".*
> 2 CORINTHIANS 6 VERSE 14

I am convinced that God listened to her concerns for me as I woke up one morning and knew I couldn't continue with this man. God had laid it on my heart that what I was doing was wrong. The relationship finished but I am happy to say we have stayed good friends.

11

THE FAMILY SECRET

It was on a trip to Scotland that I was to discover the family secret.

For years I had lived under a cloud. Why, as a child, had my father hated me so much. His violence both physically and mentally was frightening. I had never been particularly close to my siblings but having left home when I was sixteen, with enforced no contact for over two years, it wasn't surprising that there was a rift between the family and me, particularly as it was believed I had left a sinking ship. The truth was that given the choice of getting away from a fragile existence to the security of living with my beloved grandfather, there was no choice. I was unaware that bankruptcy was facing my father and only found this out many years later. We were living in a bungalow at the time, the attic of which had been boarded. Four beds were put up for my two brothers, sister and myself. There was one electric bulb hanging from a beam, no windows, no privacy and it was cold, very cold. I slept in the same vest and knickers which I had been wearing during the day, nightwear was not an option – nighties and pyjamas were luxuries that my mother could not afford. To be able to leave all this behind and join my grandfather was a dream come true.

It was only after the death of my mother and father that I began to pick up the pieces with my siblings and this has continued as we now spend time together when we can, albeit they are scattered round the globe.

❋ ❋ ❋ ❋

So it was that Grace and I had gone to Scotland to visit my great Aunt. She was getting on in age and I was keen to keep in touch with her. I had made it my business to get up to Scotland and visit her and my mother's sister if not every year, at least every other and now it was that time. It was during this visit that the family secret was finally divulged.

We met up for afternoon tea at the hotel where Grace and I were staying. Grace had gone upstairs to change and I had aged Auntie on my own. After a few more niceties Auntie was talking with great fondness about my mother when I decided to tackle her.

"Auntie, is there something you know that no-one else knows about my mother?"

I had always found it rather strange that even as a teenager this Aunt would somehow bring into the conversation the fact that my mother had been involved with another man before my father. His name was always mentioned with affection and I had learned a little about him. He was a student doctor when my mother had been going out with him and eventually became a GP. All the family seemed genuinely fond of him and his family, but my mother had met my father and that was that.

My father had told me in temper many, many times, that I wasn't his daughter but my mother had always jumped in to defend the situation and I suppose I didn't think too much of it until two incidents made me start to realise something might be amiss. I began to suspect my mother was hiding the truth from me. One incident was not long after the death of my grandfather. I was staying with a neighbour who had also been my grandmother's friend. We were preparing supper when she suddenly said "Of course, dear, you do know that your father is not really your father, don't you." I had been gob smacked but wanting not to seem a fool, I had replied that of course, I knew and the matter had been dropped. That was a mistake, so often I have wished I had asked her for more information. Then I bumped into a man at the tennis club who had known my mother. He enquired after my mother, "and your step father?" Again, feeling a bit of a fool, I didn't make more enquiries and kept quiet.

Now was my last chance. My mother and father were dead and Auntie was the only person who would know. Even my Mother's sister would have been too young to be aware and my mother, I knew, could be very secretive.

"What do you mean, dear?" She looked at me with raised eyebrows.

"Was Robert really my father?"

She looked flustered. "Well", she hesitated.

"Please tell me the truth, I have suspected for a while but I need to know. Mum and Dad are both dead now so the secret has gone to the grave; I am sure you are the only one who really knows the truth."

She sighed. "Well dear. Yes, I always believed TJ to be your father but it doesn't make sense because none of your children look Continental."

"Continental?" I nearly fell off my chair.

"Well, yes, didn't I tell you he was Italian."

This was a complete shock. I had an Italian father. It was

just then that Grace reappeared. She had tied her dark hair back and as she walked toward us I thought my Aunt was gong to faint. "Oh my, oh my" she kept saying, fanning herself, "She is the spitting image of TJ's sister."

Things were beginning to fall into place. There had been many times when both Grace and Andrew had been taken for being Spanish or Italian and I could now see the likeness. Susie was so different being very fair skinned and much like my mother's side of the family.

Auntie was very excited, it was as if she could contain herself no more and the opportunity to talk about it at last was out. Grace and I listened intently.

My mother had been going out with TJ for some time. He obviously adored my mother but she was very young still in her teens. Then she met Robert. Pregnant out of wedlock in 1939 was still seen to be shameful and my grandmother was horrified. I still think it is possible that my mother didn't know who the father was at that stage, but my grandmother was very quick to turn the situation to the family's advantage. Robert came from a good naval family. His father was a Captain in the Royal Navy and they were comfortably off. On the other hand TJ was a student but worse still an Italian and this would have been a double disgrace for the family as the Italians were supporting Germany in the unease prior to the Second World War. So my mother wed Robert in late 1939. I wouldn't say she was forced into the marriage, as I think she had fallen in love with Robert but I have no doubt he was forced into marrying my mother. Things were fine until I arrived, two months early but an obviously full term baby. It didn't take Robert long to realise he had been duped and I suppose the hatred started from that day, mostly aimed at me although my mother didn't get away lightly. As a child I used to hide under the blankets when I heard him yelling and hitting my mother, scared I was going to be next. My mother took it all and stayed with him throughout the years, partly because she had nowhere else to go but also in those days you just had to get on with it as divorce was not an easy option. Five other children were born to them but his hatred for me stayed throughout my life.

As the story unfolded, I began to sympathise with Robert. Although it was very wrong that he should have taken his aggression out on me, his life was just beginning when he was forced into the responsibility of a marriage and child. I could now feel sorry for him and thought of him as a bitter old man and no longer as the father he was supposed to be. It was like a light had come on and relief that he, in his eyes, had maybe good reason for despising me.

After we returned home Auntie and I had very many long phone calls as she recalled other incidents which she had to share with me. It was like a giant jigsaw puzzle as more and more of the pieces fitted together.

I ventured this new exciting information to my siblings but, of course, they found it difficult to accept and understand. As one of my brother's pointed out, when I visited him in Thailand last year, "Don't forget you only had 16 years with father, we had 40 and we remember him with affection and the fun we had".

The question of whether I should try and find TJ or his family is always with me and maybe I will one day. I so enjoy having the relationship I now do with my siblings that I don't want to upset the applecart but I do feel a deep affinity with Italy and Italians and, of course, my love and understanding for medicine has got to have come from somewhere. Was he sporty? As I pick up my tennis racquet, do a few lengths in the pool or remember how much I loved netball, I realise there are many more unanswered question. None of my siblings are interested in sport – my hobbies must have come from somewhere.

In the meantime I am content that at last the family secret is out and God has given me the grace and understanding to forgive Robert.

❋ ❋ ❋ ❋

EPILOGUE

Through my Bible Study Groups I have made some really treasured friends. It was at one such meeting when we were discussing how God had come into our lives that a member suggested I write about it. "Oh I couldn't," was my first reaction". I was writing children's poetry and short stories, and to start an autobiography? No, I didn't think I could. A few days later something clicked in the back of my mind. Then I remembered…

A few years previously I had started writing an autobiography but not God related. This was more to do with child abuse and I think probably to get all my horrible childhood memories exorcized through writing. I had been in touch with a retired Publisher who had taken me under his wing. He had suggested I make the book into a novel rather than an autobiography, encouraged by his interest I agreed. Every week I sent him three chapters to edit. He was very positive and we finally finished it and started sending it out to Publishers and Agents, following the guidelines of the *Writers and Artists Yearbook*. Needless to say, it was rejected, as are so many others, and then suddenly, sadly he died. There didn't seem much point in continuing and I put the manuscript on the shelf for my children or grandchildren to read in later years.

Maybe I should look at it again. I got it out and started to read it – there it was – at every turning God was in my life guiding me and I hadn't realised it. When I started meditating, the words "write" kept coming to me and I am sure this is what God wanted me to do.

Now when I feel I am walking on eggshells I pray, and I know God's hand is on my shoulder.

So, why us? Why has God showered my family with so much grace?

> **Ask, and you will receive;**
> **seek, and you will find;**
> **knock, and the door will be**
> **opened to you.**
>
> Luke 11 verse 9.

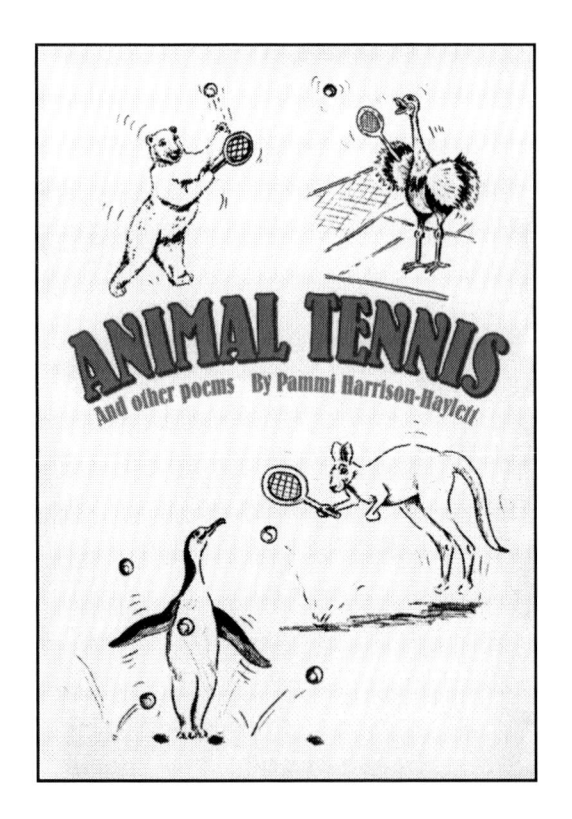

ANIMAL TENNIS AND OTHER POEMS
Pammi Harrison-Haylett

ILLUSTRATIONS BY JACKIE BOOTMAN

This collection of fun poetry has been put together in the hope that it will benefit children of all ages. The proceeds from the sales of these books and CDs will be going to Help the Hospices, in particular the Children's Hospices, the Snowdrop Trust and various other Charities for children.

By buying this book or CD, you are helping these Charities and 1 hope will have fun and enjoy these poems.

Obtainable from St Wilfred's Hospice, Chichester

ISBN 0-9541066-0-1   £5

NEW BOOTS PRESS